T0330353

The Experience Society

The Experience Society

Consumer Capitalism Rebooted

Steven Miles

First published 2021 by Pluto Press
345 Archway Road, London N6 5AA

www.plutobooks.com

British Library Cataloguing in Publication Data
A catalogue record for this book is available from the British Library

ISBN   978 0 7453 3870 5   Hardback
ISBN   978 0 7453 3869 9   Paperback
ISBN   978 1 7868 0559 1   PDF eBook
ISBN   978 1 7868 0561 4   Kindle eBook
ISBN   978 1 7868 0560 7   EPUB eBook

Typeset by Stanford DTP Services, Northampton, England

Printed and bound by CPI Group (UK) Ltd, Croydon, CR0 4YY

Contents

Preface

The Experience Society came into being in the years and months leading up to the global pandemic that was and is Covid-19. It has become conventional wisdom to suggest that as a result of Covid-19 nothing will be quite the same again and, least of all, how it is we consume. Commentators have, indeed, queued up to reflect on the widespread destruction of retail caused by the pandemic, while speculating about how our relationship to consumption might change as we gradually come to terms with whatever might become 'the new normal'. Writing in September, 2020, there is some evidence of the inkling of an economic recovery, and of consumers returning to their old habits, but the overriding suspicion is that consumption has indeed reached something of a crossroads.

Will Covid-19 reinvent what it means to be a consumer in an experience society? The lion's share of this book was written in a world that felt as though it was more manageable and understandable, one in which the impact of consumption on everyday lives was perhaps following a more predictable trajectory. However, the impact of Covid-19 may well be one in which some of the trends this book seeks to understand are intensified. *The Experience Society* speaks to a world in which the relationship between consumption and selfhood is heightened and in which human beings have, in effect, become indistinguishable from the experiences through which consumer capitalism defines them. This isn't a world in which the freedoms of consumption are liberating, but rather one in which our adherence to the social and cultural norms determined by consumer capitalism is entrenched in ever-more sophisticated ways.

Of course, the economic and cultural impacts of the virus are omnipresent. We are having to rethink our work practices and how it is we engage with leisure. Some of the experience-heavy service industries which I refer to in the course of the book appear to have been decimated by the virus. The tourism and hospitality industries have slumped, as partly demonstrated by the fact that the number of shoppers in London dropped by around a half between 2019 and 2020. Our city centres are ghosts of their former selves as consumers have apparently adjusted to a world of suburban home working and economic hardship. Pre-pandemic, 40 per cent of John Lewis's business, a key retailer in the UK, was online. By September 2020 this had risen to above 60 per cent. In April 2020 spending on hot drinks in the UK dropped by nearly 90 per cent, while in September 2020 Pret A Manger cut 3,000 jobs and closed 30 outlets. How we consume, or at least how it is we shop appears to have been transformed in a remarkably short period of time, a set of circumstances that online providers such as Amazon have been well-placed to exploit. Meanwhile, it's as if how we experience work has been propelled ten years forward: home working has become the norm overnight and office workers are unlikely to return to a world in which they are wedded to their city centre desks.

There is of course much talk of the way in which the virus has pulled the rug from under key experiential sectors such as theatre, cinema, museums and live sport. For at least the foreseeable future, any kind of direct experience of leisure is watered down by the fear of what social proximity might bring. Some have speculated that the thirst for personal experiences could, in the medium to longer term, lead to the increased popularity of immersive technologies. But what is certain is that the question of mental health and well-being is evermore under the spotlight under conditions in which social interaction is so closely regulated. In short, my contention, indeed my fear, is that Covid-19 will intensify the shift toward an experience society, thereby expediting the ability of consumer capitalism to exploit this transition to its own ends. The more isolated Covid-19 makes us feel the more we lust after the sense of self that we imagine experiences can bring us.

This all reflects a state of affairs that I will argue fashions our understanding of the ways consumer capitalism obliges us to behave, while simultaneously making us more vulnerable to such processes. The Experience Society puts the onus on the individual to feel that they belong and to demonstrate his or her feeling of belonging so that in effect the self becomes the conduit for this process. It's in this light that Jia Tolentino (2019) talks about the process of optimisation in her book, *Trick Mirror: Reflection on Self-Delusion*. We consume as a means of optimising our performance while ensuring this is reinforced through our appearance which maximises the effect. The point here is that the impact of Covid-19 is not to temper the impact of experiential forms of consumption on who we are. To argue as much would imply that consumption itself only has an impact on those who can afford a fully-fledged consumer lifestyle. Indeed, there might well be an argument for saying the opposite: the less you have the means to consume the more important consumption is for both the way you see yourself and your ability to be included in a society that puts so much onus on the status-bearing qualities of consumption.

It is for the above reason that Covid-19 doesn't actually change anything, at least in an ideological sense. What it does do is intensify the consumer-driven state of affairs we already found ourselves in prior to lockdown. In this sense the new-normal is looking suspiciously like the old normal. In an ideal world we might like to imagine that this is the beginning of the end of the consumer society: that if any good comes out of Covid-19 it might be the realisation that we need to change our ways and that uncommodified communal experiences might be the way forward.

Covid-19 has created a moment in history, where, given the impact of lockdown and of social distancing globally, who we are and how it is we understand ourselves becomes ever more visceral and immediate. While I run the risk of appearing overly pessimistic here, the chances of this sense of amplified being actually facilitating the emergence of a brave new world remains, realistically, remote. The innate need that human beings have to feel part of something, and to feel that they have some semblance of control over what it means to be them, is something that consumer capitalism will continue to greedily exploit. Covid-19 may well ensure that such needs are magnified to the nth degree and for that reason the experience society will have more of a hold on us today and tomorrow than it ever did in the more carefree world of the past.

1

Introducing the Experience Society

Experience is the new ideological terrain of the consumer society. We live in a world in which consumption is less and less about the 'using up' and 'laying to waste' of products and more and more about the maximisation of the moment; about the ephemera of an experience planted in the human imagination. The success of consumer capitalism has long depended on its ability to reinvent itself. This can at least in part be described as a transition from the consumption of needs to the consumption of wants. In this book, I will argue that this process has graduated onto the consumption of experiences. This is not, in itself, a revelation. Many commentators have considered the role of experience in the reproduction of the so-called 'experience economy' (Sundbo and Sørensen, 2013). However, what has tended to be neglected in this discussion is the ideological dimensions of this process and what it tells us about what it really means to be a citizen of a consumer society. *The Experience Society* seeks to understand an ever more sophisticated reimagineering of capitalism and hence, of an ideological process in which what and how we consume as citizens of a consumer society actively defines who and what it is we are. The experience society brings us closer to a sense of belonging to a world where such a sense feels harder to come by. And yet it simultaneously takes that belonging completely out of our grasp. In *The Experience Society* I will hence argue that the acceleration of forms of experiential consumption necessitate nothing less than a root and branch reconsideration of the social scientific significance of what it means to consume.

Ideology Reimagined

The ideological foundations that underpin consumer capitalism and the role it plays in forging a political imaginary have long been a matter of fascination. In a neoliberal context it can be argued that the values of the market and of private property have come to be absolute and that democracy has effectively been reinvented as the ability to consume. What this represents is a shift of liberty from the political to the economic where the market determines who wins and who loses (Brown, 2015). The all-powerful nature of a neoliberal rationality inevitably produces an unequal society and a form of citizenship that is defined above all by the access, or otherwise, to consumption, for it is consumption that defines the 'good life'. There is an irony here. That is, the more neoliberalism reconstructs human beings as forms of human capital as Brown suggests, the more it questions the value of the individual as an arbiter of his or her own future; the more he or she looks to consumption as a means of finding him or herself, and the more his or herself is lost.

I want to present the argument here that consumption is essentially a psycho-social phenomenon. Herein lies its power. What I mean by that is that its effects are not purely sociological or purely psychological in nature, as academic boundaries insist on implying, but they constitute a complex interaction of the two. This is a position that has been hinted at in the literature (see e.g. Gabriel and Lang, 2016) but one that has rarely been executed or fully explored. That consumption is the phenomenon by which the individual consumer, regardless of his or her ability (or the extent of their resources) to consume, comes to belong to the society in which he or she lives (see Bauman, 1998), a process that in turn mediates, to put this in a somewhat old-fashioned way, the relationship between structure and agency. The consumer society coerces consumers into behaving in particular ways. It ties them to the society in which they live while convincing them that the arena of consumption not only constitutes a 'natural' state of affairs but can also provide them with the sense of belonging and freedom that other aspects of social life simply cannot.

It's in the above light that Uusitalo (1998) contends that consumption reflects a combination of the universal need to establish difference alongside the parallel need to establish strong identifying relationships. What's important here, given the time at which Uusitalo was writing and the penchant at the time for discussing the fragmented nature of post-modern identities, is the recognition that reality is fundamentally mediated. This in turn hints at Baudrillard's (1991) vision of hyper-reality and the sense that the world of social interaction is at best of a quasi-nature (see also Thompson, 1990). The work of Baudrillard is prescient in this context insofar as he identifies the emergence of a society driven by a consumer logic: an age of simulation and simulacra in which nothing is real or authentic. As Stebbins (2009) recognises, in Baudrillard's world how we consume becomes more important than how we produce, in the sense that society is geared up to produce goods to meet the 'ideological genesis of needs' (Baudrillard, 1991). Baudrillard thus discusses the triumph of a signifying culture in which culture, previously determined, is now free floating and determining: the product of a cynical parody of media images (see also Featherstone, 1991). Most crucial perhaps, for Baudrillard at least, is the point that it is via advertising and marketing that the consumer society is fuelled, and not least by the relentless promotion of the idea that through it happiness and satisfaction can be achieved. The point here is that such happiness is not about any kind of *deep* inner enjoyment, but about the visibility of attained enjoyment through the shared display of signs and consumption. This then is a kind of 'enforced happiness' contrived by the market to ensure that the consumer is constantly reminded about his or her own needs and how these needs can be met through the opportunity to consume.

The transition to which I refer is one in which the self is commodified. But in a way that is far more intense than it would have been in the past. I will deal with this issue most directly in Chapter 2, but my point is that in order to achieve the above sense of happiness, however partial it might be, a conjoining of intense subjectivism alongside a simultaneous objectivism takes place (Illouz, 2007). This amounts to a reaching within the self, but only through the predefined routes that consumer capitalism provides. In many senses, this process and the feelings it engenders can be said to have been accentuated in the past 20 or so years, not least in light of the emergence of digital mediation and social media. What I'm identifying here is a tension; a tension between a society that at least on the surface demands that you belong, alongside an analogous intensification of selfhood. The point here is that this isn't just the product of a new technologically driven economic order that perpetuates consumption in ever new forms, but of a broader process of ideological evolution (see Jameson, 1991).

It is important to remember that consumption isn't solely about the freedom of choice or indeed about the expression of fragmented identities. As Uusitalo (1998) notes, consumption has come to play an increasingly key role in the structuring of society in a world in which the integrative power of work (and indeed class) has apparently been diminished. Such trends are part of a broader process in which the success of capitalism is entirely dependent upon its ability to reinvent itself. Modernity was all about the thirst for progress, about the ability of human beings to create a world in their own guise: an instrumental world that would be capable of serving the common interest. But modernity failed. That ambition was never met and what arguably emerged instead was a fragmentary and a highly divided world in which belonging came to be defined by the ability to consume (see Bauman, 1998) and by capitalism's ability to reboot by reinventing how people consumed.

Uusitalo (1998) points out that in a post-industrial society production and consumption are dissolving into each other so that, in effect, products become indistinguishable from their marketing. It's in a similar way that consumers have become indistinguishable from their experiences. The changing nature of consumption is not something that can be contained. It has a fundamental impact on how we experience society and how society, at least symbolically, experiences us. But the concern here is that the new kind of bonds that this society creates are inevitably partial. What we consume and how we consume it in an experience society may bring us together, but it does this in a momentary fashion and in that moment we are bonded above all to the economic system that defines us. It is this process that I argue sits at the heart of social change today.

The amplification of experience could be said to reflect a long-term transition in the consumers' relationship to consumption from that of a process of self-production rather than one of self-distinction (Uusitalo, 1998); something that was long ago identified by Marx (1989: 94) who, far from focusing solely on consumption as distribution and exchange, saw consumption as a form of self-restoration: 'The individual produces an object, and by consuming it, returns to himself, but returns as a productive and self-reproducing individual.' For Marx, it was the combination of commodity fetishism and alienated labour that constituted the ideology of capitalism. The working classes were unwilling to engage in revolution because they were more caught up in 'a nexus of false ideas'. Thus Heath and Potter (2005: 23) describe a state of affairs in which the working classes came to be preoccupied with incremental gains, as opposed to revolution, and as a result were simply 'redecorating the cage in which they were imprisoned'. It was in this context, argue Heath and Potter (2005), that Marxism came to rethink the notion of ideology, not least through the work of Gramsci (2005), who argued that capitalism wilfully created a false consciousness through a complete cultural hegemony, a world of cultural products which as long as they existed would simply serve to reflect and reinforce bourgeois ideologies. Heath and Potter's (2005) critique of Marxist approaches is interesting here insofar as it highlights some of the tensions that exist around the role of consumption in social change. If the problem with capitalism was that it exploited the working classes and in the process created poverty and suffering why shouldn't culture and indeed forms of popular consumption provide a way out in this regard?

> It was precisely the failure of the capitalist system to provide the workers with goods that gave them the reason to overthrow the system in the first place. Thus the critique of consumerism comes perilously close to criticising capitalism for satisfying the workers *too much*. They're stuffed, they can't be bothered to go out and overthrow the system anymore. But this poses the question: why would they want to? (Heath and Potter, 2005: 33)

There is something to be said for this argument. But perhaps what it does neglect is the psycho-social dimension of consumption. In his work Adorno (1991a) basically argues that exchange value has come to supplant use value. The working classes effectively desire the very deceptions that consumption depends upon even though they are transparent to them. We can knowingly consume a product precisely because we do not feel duped by it; we desire it despite the duping (Cremin, 2011). The way we seek to go about defining ourselves through consumption has certainly changed through time, and this book is thus concerned with the way this has helped to intensify the ideological power of consumer capitalism. Indeed, as Salecl (2011) has argued, in a world characterised by a need for constant self-improvement, in a world in which the orthodoxy of choice remains largely unspoken, and unreal and yet assumed, we become the victims of a way of self-perception in which we are, perhaps regrettably, the masters of our own fate. We feel that we can 'choose'.

In today's society which glorifies choice and the idea that choice is always in people's interests, the problem is not just the scale of choice available but the manner in which choice is represented. Life choices are described in the same terms as consumer choices: we set out to find the right life as we would the right kind of wallpaper or hair conditioner ... the problem is that the idea of rational choice, transferred from the domain of economics, has been glorified as the only kind of choice we have. (Salecl, 2011: 8)

This sense of choice is not just about goods or services; it's about the ability to choose our selves given that, as the sports brand Adidas put it, 'Impossible is Nothing'. As citizens of a consumer society we live in a whirlwind of perpetual choice, whether it be in education, health, housing or countless other realms. But the ability to choose is transmuted into an ideology of the self-made (wo)man so that we convince ourselves that life is about a series of options and potential transformations, despite the fact that the society in which we live legislates against this. One author that has sought to understand the impact of social change on the self is Elemer Hankiss (2006), who argues that the syncretic civilisation of the consumer age constitutes an age of paradox in which we are experiencing the apotheosis of the human personality and its simultaneous annihilation:

It is the Me Age and the Age of the No-Self at the same time. Seen from one angle, it is the age of triumphant self-actualization, of radical individualism, an age when the human person has become the object of cult and the ultimate source of values. Yet, from the opposite angle, we witness the self's destruction. (Hankiss, 2006: 197–8)

The problem for Hankiss is that at a time of rapid social change when the individual is bewildered by a sense of uncertainty and self-blame, his or her responsibility for self-direction is intensified, thereby diluting any sense of freedom they might 'experience' along the way. In an increasingly (apparently) godless world, where traditional sources of purpose and meaning are in rapid decline, he or she becomes the ultimate, perhaps the only, arbiter of his or her own meaning. The implications of this for our understanding of the experience society is the increased value of time so that our experience of the world is lived through precious moments of intensity. Indeed,

> hundreds of millions of people … are looking for an ultimate source of life and meaning in the moment. And consumer civilization provides them, around the clock, with myriad intense and significant moments (or at least with the illusion that they experience these significant moments) … Consumer civilization, for its part, offers people some help. It makes them feel the beauty of the moment, and the serenity of eternity, and it generates in them the illusion that these two, the moment and the eternity, unite in a beautiful harmony. (Hankiss, 2006: 214)

Hankiss goes as far as to describe this as an age of experience, a world without transcendence where everything needs to be experienced to the full: a necessity if people's existential fears and anxieties are to be assuaged or if they are to be 'dazzled and immunized' against the growing fears of the emerging civilisation. It's here that the human imagination steps in. By focusing on the impossibility of the 'good life', the currency that consumption provides becomes essential and that life is defined by the resources we need in order to reassure ourselves that we belong (see Tuan, 1998). Consumption is thus our escape into a world better imagined. In a sense then, the world of commodified experience in which we find ourselves so readily immersed today is the product of a long-term historical process in which the self has become increasingly separated from the world, despite a feeling of the polar opposite. We are independent and yet isolated to the extent that we are obliged to define our own worlds. It's this paradox that ensures consumption plays such a pivotal role in the world in which we live, however much our cultural capital leads us to deny as much. Robert David Sack (1992) thus argues that the glittering realm of consumption appears to offer us a world 'without constraints and without responsibility', a disorienting world in which the consequences of our actions are obscured through our emphasis on a front stage without a back stage to prop it up. The world of experience is both an escape and a means of propping up the self; of legitimising its morality, in Sack's (1992) terms, and of giving it a voice and a kind of stability which it effectively took away from us in the first place. The consumption of experience gives and it takes away.

What is Experience?

So what is experiential consumption and how has it become so important to how the consumer relates to the society in which he or she lives? There has been a tradition in cultural and consumer studies of critically engaging with products that may or may not tell us something insightful about the relationship between a consumer artefact, consumption and social change (see Du Gay et al., 1996; Miller and Woodward, 2012). Clearly there is an experience, or indeed experiences, involved in consuming such products that, not least insofar as how we consume them, may serve to connect us to the world around us. For example, today we do not consume an iPhone solely on the basis of its functional attributes and quality. We do so, at least partly, because the ownership of the iPhone says something about our discernment as consumers, and more importantly implies that we belong in the same ways as those around us who are also consuming the iPhone, belong. The power of the iPhone lies at least partly in its symbolism: what its ownership says about its owner. This provides us with a form of capital that in turn appeases the jagged edges that would otherwise appear in our social relations should we 'choose' to consume an 'inferior' brand. The added value that such products embody in version after version after updated version, have long been at the heart of how consumer capitalism reinvents itself.

Nobody actually needs the choice of thousands of car models or indeed, as Miller and Woodward (2012) point out, the apparently endless range of styles of jeans that the market makes available to them. However, this form of commodity exchange is limited in the sense that at least consumers' need for products is finite. Someone may have 200 pairs of training shoes in their collection. They are less likely to own 200 iPhones. The process that this implies is also fairly primitive and steeped in historical precedence. But the emergence of a world of digital consumption and a world that is increasingly deterritorialised in the sense that how you consume is less and less determined by the physical space in which you consume, have arguably created a space for a radically different kind of consumption, one in which experience is much more at the heart of why and how we consume. Airbnb, gaming, escape rooms, Premier League football, craft beer, the revitalisation of live comedy and music, celebrity restaurants, themed restaurants, theme parks, Amazon, eBay, all-in holidays, cruise ships, box sets, Netflix (and possibly chill).

These are all examples of experiential forms of consumption in which the power of the product to impact upon your life is intensified by your ability as a consumer to effectively add your own value, to bring the product to life through the narrative that you and apparently only you can bring to it. Let me offer a further example. At the time of writing, and from a mere £162, you can buy a ticket to Mamma Mia! The Party: 'Created by ABBA's Björn Ulvaeus, Mamma Mia! The Party is a new and unique entertainment experience that puts you in the heart of the action. Over the course of more than five hours, you'll enjoy a spectacular show, a three-course gourmet Mediterranean meal and an ABBA disco all in one unforgettable evening' (Mamma Mia!, 2019). Such an event is characterised by many of the key dimensions of an experience society. The event is explicitly about self-gifting. The consumer isn't simply an observer but an active participant, in this case in an escapist world of music-driven nostalgia. This is experience manufactured. And it is more than escape. It is in essence a process of self-illusory validation.

The emergence of experience as an essential characteristic of how people consume is not accidental. It is at least partly the product of an economic strategy. Indeed, for Pine and Gilmore (1999) the future health of the economy depends on the effective staging of memorable events. For them, experiences must be memorable and powerful if the consumer is to be an active participant in the event in which they are immersed. What sells is not a product or service, but the experience attached to that product or service (Klingmann, 2007). For example, in Chapter 8 I focus on the coffee shop experience, which is about far more than the straightforward drinking of a beverage, but is all about the transformation of a single commodity (coffee) into a comprehensive setting (the coffee shop) that adds up to more than the value of its parts. In an experience society everything is potentially better presented and received as an experience, not only of media and commercial forms of consumption, but also culture and education, so that a visit to the museum, for example, is a symbiotic process of production and consumption. Such environments are ripe for cognitive interpretation insofar as they, 'Show rather than tell, delight rather than instruct' (Klingmann, 2007: 42).

But there is something more fundamental going on here. The word experience implies a degree of agency, and yet experiences are highly produced, industrially so, in fact (O'Sullivan and Spangler, 1999). The tension that exists here is all about the extent to which experience is choreographed or produced and the ability of the consumer to define it for themselves. O'Sullivan and Spangler do well to dwell on some of the psychological elements of experiential consumption, going as far as to argue that experiences serve 'the psychic needs of a society' (1999: 4), but they do so in such a way as to imply that these elements are above all *manufactured*: that the marketer effectively has the power to conduct the consumer in order that he or she can procure psychological benefits from their consumption experience. What I want to explore in this book is something a little different: the idea that the new evolving world of consumption is less about the *production* of experience and more about how such experience encourages us to *feel* that we have more control and that what we are controlling here are physical, mental or emotional moments. These are moments that on the one hand appear to free us up, but on the other hand tie us to the ideologies of consumer capitalism in ways that are perhaps more binding than they ever were in the past. It is via this means that consumer capitalism has effectively been rebooted. The consumer capitalism we live by is a consumer capitalism in which the self is centre stage, but in which in any kind of a centring of the self is little more than a façade designed to reaffirm their lived commitment to a social and economic system that equates choice with freedom.

Private Experience; Public Self

It is important to note that I am not arguing that the new mode of consumption automatically make consumers active participants in their consumption experiences, but rather that it propagates the *sense* that this is the case. That in short, this age of experience (not least that promoted by the sense of freedom consumers can now access digitally) revitalises the ideological potential of consumer capitalism through the illusory plane of self-expression that experience provides. Thus, the vision of an active form of consumption that authors such as Pine and Gilmore (1999) promote could be said to be unconvincing in the sense that the production of situations in which consumers do appear to be more proactive may do nothing more than intensify their passivity.

As I noted above, the notion of an experience society isn't entirely unique. Indeed, the German sociologist Gerhard Schulze identified the existence of such an entity back in 1995 with a book of the same name.

For Schulze the experience society is defined by an underlying shift from consumption being a means to resolve external issues (e.g. buying a caravan as a means of leisure transport) to it being about satisfying the ideas he or she has about him or herself (buying a caravan to fulfil a notion of self as travelled and fully leisured). This transition brings with it a certain concentrated quality. Through their changing relationship with consumption consumers are no longer playing the long game; they are living for the moment and making the absolute most of that moment. In effect life becomes an experiential project. It is no longer, from this perspective, about getting on and through life, but about designing it for their own best interests. Experiences are made and not received. What's interesting about Schulze's analysis is the implication that there is a degree of instrumentalisation going on here. The consumer has an internal goal. They actively use experience as a means of achieving a subjective end. The subject digests situations in order to convert them into intensely singular (i.e. subjectively determined) experiences. The irony is that in engaging in such experiences the individual helps to maintain a society in which experience homogenises. The consumer feels liberated, in control, but that sense of control serves a bigger purpose.

Various authors have, of course, commented on how the society in which we live has become increasingly atomised and alienating and that in this context the world of consumption steps in to provide us with a source of meaning; a sense of exultation perhaps. For Thrift (2006: 85), for example, the process of commodification is about constructing and marketing the products which meet these needs the most. From this point of view experiences and events (and not least mega-events – see Chapter 3) serve the purpose of making attendees believe that they are 'doing something amazing (so they return in future years), yet that something is actually a hyper-real, fake, watered-down version of the original experience, because the mega-event is controlled by the entertainment industries, which are key components of the culture industry'. This is just one example (and many others will be considered during the course of this book) of how contemporary consumer capitalism convinces us of our uniqueness and in doing so ties us to the social system that controls us. As consumer citizens we are arguably complicit in the manufacture of an experience society.

What is effectively being described here is a process in which over time a new individualism has emerged. Such individualism is the product of a capitalism that has sought to expand its influence through a focus on identity needs and the search for meaning that this implies (Lodziak, 1995). Authors such as Curtis (2013) have more recently described a process whereby the market of neoliberalism has become a kind of undisputed common sense, or a way of being, a form of 'idiotism'. For Curtis, idiotism is all about the privatisation of life, a process that results in human beings being atomised as relentlessly self-interested individuals. This amounts to a 'capturing of the soul' in which everything and anything of a creative or imaginative bent is set to work in the best interests of generating economic value (Berardi, 2009). The world that Berardi describes is a world in which the personalisation of culture, a new version of publicness, has emerged in which 'mind-share' is an end goal. The culture in which we live, from this point of view, as perhaps exemplified by the world of celebrity culture and of social media, is about negating privacy and yet valorising it at one and the same time. How we see ourselves thus becomes the product of a process of performance and display through which the soul is mined (Curtis, 2013).

Theoretical Roots

At this stage I want to take a couple of steps back in order to consider two of the most important of all contributions to discussions around the ideological context in which consumption operates. Specifically, I want to consider what these two approaches might tell us about the question of satisfaction that I mentioned in the context of the work of Schulze (1995) above. Key here then is both the work of the Frankfurt School, specifically of Horkheimer and Adorno, and that of Debord (1995) and in particular his discussion of the society of the spectacle. Horkheimer and Adorno are commonly seen to represent the consumer as a passive entity; the mirror to market forces that obliges them to behave in particular ways (see Ransome, 2005). What is perhaps at the core of their position is the recognition that capitalism came to dominate not simply through the economic, but via the cultural realm so that docile forms of consumerism reinforced the status quo and reinforced the powerlessness of the masses. And herein lies the rub: the more the apparent benefits of consumerism appeal to the consumer the more the ideological power of consumer capitalism is free to assert its authority (something I will go on to discuss in the context of experience as this book progresses). For Horkheimer and Adorno (1972) the key transition in the evolution of the authority of capitalism lies in its ability to dissipate any sense of a common identity in consumers. Consumption and the freedoms it allegedly implies is thus depolitcising, while the superficial benefits of consumption come at a significant cost: that of the loss of mental freedom (see also Marcuse, 2002). The term 'culture industry' reflects Horkheimer and Adorno concern that mass culture does not arise spontaneously from the masses, but is foisted upon them in a calculated fashion to the extent that, 'The customer is not king as the culture industry would like to have us believe, not its subject but its object' (Adorno, 1989: 129). The stranglehold that consumption has over us is built upon the thirst for satisfaction that it inspires; and the fact that such satisfaction is little more than an impossible dream:

> The culture industry perpetually cheats its consumers of what it perpetually promises. The promisory note, with its plots and staging, it draws on pleasure, is endlessly prolonged, the promise, which is actually all the spectacle consists of, is illusory: all it actually confirms is that the real point will never be reached, that the diner must be satisfied with the menu. (Horkheimer and Adorno, 1972: 139)

Consumption is effectively standardised and as such it reflects the economic rationality of production more broadly (see Lodziak, 2002). Consumption is formulaic: it self-consciously appeals to the common denominator so that its products are designed not to satisfy, but rather to prevent audiences from becoming bored. Audiences are indeed flattered by the fact they enjoy the consumption of a particular form of popular music, radio, film or television. Repetition is both reassuring and comforting. In this respect consumption constitutes a form of propaganda capable of proficiently sustaining the status quo while diverting the masses from their common goals (Lodziak, 2002).

There is a long-term debate as to whether or not the above should lead us to conclude that Horkheimer and Adorno are in the business of condemning consumers as little more than mindless dupes, Edwards (2000) going as far as to contend that their patronising view of consumers is a 'near-Armageddon-like' killing off, or at least undermining of, the human subject. Lodziak (2002) thus questions a tendency to suggest that consumption is produced by advertising and the media, when the position of the Frankfurt School is actually more aligned to an understanding of consumption as the product of the alienation of labour and the impact of this on the organisation and experience of employment. In other words, the problem here is not so much the mass production facilitated by the media, but the fact that this is in itself the product of a process which cuts off the producer from his product. We are thus obliged to consume goods in order to meet our basic human needs. It is the ability of the capitalist system to organise how we meet our needs that makes the worker powerless, a position that was equally evident in the work of André Gorz (1967).

But what's more important to contemplate for the purposes of this book, is the idea that the reinvention of consumption as experience effectively increases and intensifies the parameters within which the consumer is obliged to be satisfied with the menu that Horkheimer and Adorno (1972) describe above. For Horkheimer and Adorno entertainment cannot offer genuine escape; for that escape can never be anything more than an escape from the idea that such resistance can be achieved (Horkheimer and Adorno, 1972; see also Wilson, 2007). And in an echo of Weber's (2002) work, even self-preservation becomes self-destructive. Returning to the broader point here, what Adorno (and Horkheimer) do so effectively is to consider the psychodynamics of popular mass culture and its role in perpetuating an isolated and atomised kind of individuality (see Dunn, 2008) so that ultimately the individual is the result of a set of social relations and not an active participant in the consumption of the images that these social relations produce. The world of experience which we appear to have entered reinforces the relationship between the two and in doing so further enhances the potential for ideological conformity.

This sense of conformity can only be fully understood in the context of a society that is increasingly geared up to the spectacular economic and cultural possibilities therein implied. As such, for the purposes of our understanding of the emergence of an experience society, the work of Guy Debord (1995) is worth reflecting upon alongside that of the Frankfurt School. Indeed, there are similarities insofar as both approaches seek to present a critical theory that puts culture at the heart of debates around the ideology of consumer capitalism (Jappe, 1999). In his seminal work, *The Society of the Spectacle*, Debord (1995) suggests that the world has devolved into what amounts to 'an immense accumulation of images' and that it had effectively become a sequence of commercial fragments detached from original experience (see Rockwell, 2006).

For Debord the spectacle lies at the heart of the capitalist system and thus plays a key role in ensuring the maintenance of consumerism as a way of life (Miles, 1998). Spectacle is effectively the product of a process of capital accumulation: the world in which we engage is effectively the world of the commodity. The spectacle can be understood in the context of a debased culture, the rise of celebrity and the underlying condition of a bureaucratic society; in light of the creation of false conflicts; and as part of the perpetual reinvention of the commodity form and as a denial of individual autonomy (Hetherington, 2007: 39). In short, the relationship between culture and the economy has been reinvented by a shift in the production and consumption of images so that, in effect, culture loses its autonomy and becomes nothing more than an appendage to an economic system in which mass production and mass marketing are ever more fundamental. As Debord (1995: 117) puts it, 'The whole life of those societies in which modern conditions of production prevail presents itself as an immense accumulation of *spectacles*. All that once was directly lived has become mere representation.' The consequence of all this is an 'objective force' in which the social relationships between people are now mediated, first and foremost, by images. What is perhaps most important about all this is Debord's notion that the spectacle constitutes just one moment in the development of commodity production (Jappe, 1999). So in other words, it is less the case that the production of spectacle governs the process of commodity production and more the case that it plays a pivotal role at the point in history which Debord describes.

One of the most effective attempts to apply Debord's theory of the spectacle and indeed debates around the spectacular nature of post-modern life is that of Krier and Swart (2016; see also Chapter 3), who argue that the post-modern economy erodes social bonds and replaces them with illusory 'commodified mechanisms for social solidarity' (2016: 3) so that the social world in which we live in is characterised less and less by social interaction and more and more by collective inner-passivity (see Žižek, 2006). In presenting their analysis, Krier and Swart (2016) discuss the contemporary relevance of Debord and in doing so argue that the society of the spectacle is a society of illusion: the more people consume the more they are disconnected from one another to the extent that the ultimate effect of the carnivalesque is social and psychological isolation, a kind of permanent dwelling in a socially bereft unreality. In a way it is this very estrangement that sits at the heart of this book. The contention being made here is that a world of apparently ever-expanding opportunities for consumption and self-exploration is not only ideologically powerful but also only partial in the degree to which the experiences it provides can serve to fulfil the needs of their 'author'. As such, the potential for alienating the consumer is ever increased. Experience is thus less about enjoyment and more about the anxiety-inducing obligations implied by the world of experience and its focus on achieving an end goal loosely defined as happiness. The problem here is that play and happiness are themselves appropriated for the uses of surplus value. They are accessed through work and bought as a form of commodified consumption (Cremin, 2011). It's for this reason that the experience society squeezes the pleasure, the spontaneity, out of what it means to be a consumer, and in the process intensifies the way in which the consumer's life is lived *psychically*. For Krier and Swart this implies a life of envious passivity, of endless promise, but of less and less fulfilment. Perhaps controversially, we could say that the world that authors like Horkheimer and Adorno (1972) described is nearer to being a reality than ever before. For Marx the fetishised nature of an exchangeable commodity depends on the maintenance of some semblance of use value to consumers. For Adorno, mass culture erodes this necessity: 'The more inexorably the principle of exchange value destroys use value for human beings, the more deeply does exchange value disguise itself as the object of enjoyment' (Adorno, 1991b: 39). This process is further intensified by the experience society, not because it is in any way more uniform or prescribed, but because consumers are more malleable to the psycho-social effects of experiences that speak to a more personalised form of prestige.

Conclusion

It is the psycho-social dimension of the experience society that makes a critical evaluation of the ideological impact of consumption so essential. Yet, up to now social scientific analyses of experience have been few and far between. One of the few recent efforts to understand the grounded and embedded nature of subjective experience is that of Scott Lash. Lash's (2018) contribution is notable for its abstraction and for the fact that at times it feels a world away from what it actually might mean to experience the everyday power dimensions through which capitalism is reproduced. However, there are elements of Lash's analysis that provide food for thought. He describes experience as the 'way we as particular individuals encounter things' (2018: 2) and notes that if there is a dominant ideology underpinning capitalism today, it is that human beings are utility-maximisng animals. This is something that is all-pervasive and naturalised. We are, as Lash puts it, self-interested, strategic and calculated beings. But there is also a sense that under such conditions each of us is out to achieve the good life to which I refer above. There are certain measurements of life in a capitalist society that we are collectively obliged to aspire to. These might include: achieving qualifications, securing a good job, marrying, having children, buying and setting up a family home, having a successful and ideally lucrative career, retiring (ideally to the south of France) and of course leaving a financial legacy to the aforementioned family. This in effect *is* the good life. And the vehicle through which we express our successful participation in the good life is consumption, not least because, as Lash suggests, the way you recognise difference, and hence a person's credentials for belonging, is via mutual recognition, and thus experience. Our belonging is defined and brought to life by how we experience such things. However, the nature of belonging is highly complex. It's important to remember that this isn't a one-way street. The world of consumption isn't simply about control. We live in a world that tends towards homogenisation, but one of the characteristics of that world is that we retain some kind of use value in our daily life routines. In this sense how we belong is inevitably 'performed' (Willis, 1991). Willis uses the example of attending a historical theme park (see Chapter 3) where the audience effectively joins actors on a stage. It is through such devices that what is actually a site of production is experienced as a commodity; and often a commodity through which the individual him or herself can be understood. Such a performance not only gives the individual consumer a setting for an experiential exploration of self, but it also negates the work and indeed the alienation that underpins it (Willis, 1991). Everything is packaged, as Willis put it, but such packaging camouflages what lies beneath the surface and reinforces the potential for our own consumerist *malaise*, the end product of which seems to be a determination to feel noticed in an era that is characterised by homogenised anonymity, 'The relentlessly positive individualist message of special allows for a world where nobody is ever ugly or sick; nobody needs to change an unhealthy lifestyle; all you have to do is find the right story to tell, the right image of yourself to reflect back through your mind's eye' (Niedzviecki, 2006: 23).

We live in a world in which we are preoccupied by the need to belong. Liberated by our breaking away from the sentimental traditions of religion, community and indeed family, we simply want to be noticed for what and who we feel we are. We live in a world of perpetual reinvention: we are always one experience away from the reinvention of a 'perfect' self (Niedzviecki, 2006). Consumption is thus more than about purchase and display, its meaningfulness arguably lies in the 'engineering of embodied experiences' (Paterson, 2006: 90), experiences that encourage anything from discipline and control (e.g. in a gym) to carnivalesque transgression. This brings us back to the suggestion that consumption is perhaps above all a mental process. However much we might seek to belong or impress through what we consume, the process of consumption weds us to a state of constant anticipation, desire and fantasy (see Campbell, 1987). But such fantasising is founded in the real, it's about imagining who and what we are and can be, which is of course the function or at least the process that advertising takes us through (Paterson, 2006). Consumption is, in short, founded upon a sense of longing, not reason (Slater, 1997).

All this is about more than the presentation and representation of a service economy. We are no longer simply interested in the consumption of tangible goods. Fantasy is everything. The consumer society packages a world of experience for us in such a way that we are at the epicentre of our own worlds. As a young boy I used to imagine that the world around me was solely there for my own purposes. That my reality was a reality of *Truman Show*-like proportions. Who and what I was, was the product of a world there solely for my own sake. And this is the very experience that the consumer society obliges us all to have. The experience society is a society characterised by the illusion of a self realised to the full: a society of spectacle brought to life through partial moments of self-satisfaction. In the remainder of *The Experience Society* I will therefore critically discuss the significance of experience in underpinning what it means to 'belong' to a consumer society. Specifically, I will consider the suggestion that what we might call a 'ramping up' of experiential forms of consumption in recent decades has intensified the ideological power of consumer capitalism; that experience transforms the nature of the relationship between structure and agency in a consumer society, and more specifically puts the psycho-social at the very heart of what it means to consume so that the self is made more vulnerable as a result. To this end I will consider a number of dimensions of the experience society. In Chapter 2 I will thus consider further the relationship between experience and identity before considering how the experience society has reimagined the consumer's experience of a number of key areas of social life, namely: leisure, work, technology, place and space, sport and, more specifically, the heightened experience of the coffee shop.

In his book *Against Everything* the cultural commentator Mark Greif (2017) suggests that we live in a world in which the more we experience, the more we are actually dissatisfied. Greif argues that experience is fundamental to how society operates today insofar as it provides something we can aspire to and attain. Happiness is intangible. Experiences are real. But there is a problem with putting experience at the heart of how we live because the more you amass experiences, the more you realise that they are less than the sum of their parts. What experience effectively does then is provide us with a taste of another life: a hint at an alternative leisured existence that is more distant from reality than ever before. Experiences are brief and potentially isolating as they oblige us to think about how different they feel from the mundane everyday.

The Experience Society asks you, the reader, to reflect on what it means to live in a society that creates an essentially unhealthy relationship with experience; a society which convinces us that an experience can be owned and realised by the sovereign individual. But the truth is that our society only truly values experience if it is paid for. The manifestations and consequences of such a state of affairs will be explored in the pages to come. The more active we feel our experiences might be, the more we open ourselves up to the ideological juggernaut that is consumer capitalism. The experience society is a world founded upon notions of feeling and thought (Wilson, 2007). But the more we think it, the less we can feel it, so that what we consume becomes less and less significant compared to *how* we consume it. The end result is that we ourselves become responsible for the very ideological parameters that could be said to determine us. And in this sense, we as citizens of the experience society are responsible for the rebooting of consumer capitalism.

2

Consumption, Identity, Experience

The question of identity has long been at the heart of debates regarding the everyday impact, influence and power of consumer capitalism. The ideological pull of consumption effectively lies in the ability of consumer goods to play a significant role in how an individual navigates and constructs his or her everyday life. The success of consumerism 'as a way of life' resides at least partially in the ability of consumer lifestyles to impart influence on our lives without us actually discerning or believing that it is doing so. In other words, consumption is ideological: it presents itself as a natural state of affairs, and we as willing consumers unwittingly accept, and indeed are arguably complicit in, the process. We reproduce the world of consumption that so readily frustrates us. The onset of the experience society compounds and exacerbates this process. The thesis underpinning this book is that this process has not only intensified the relationship between consumption and identity but, to coin a phrase, it has 'turbo charged' it, in such a way as to make consumers ever more susceptible to the power that consumer capitalism imparts.

It is important to remember, however, that the above transition is part of a much longer process. Yes, broadly speaking, we might reflect upon the possibility that how we consume has become increasingly significant as a marker of our social, cultural and even psychological 'habitus', as other elements in our social life have become less dependable and more uncertain. We might also reflect on the notion that the consumption-based experiences we have today play a more important part in who we are than how and what specific objects we consume. But this transition can only be understood as part of the evolution of a much more profound process in which the influences on what and how we consume have become more sophisticated in *how* they affect our sense of self than they would have been in the past. In this chapter I will consider what it is that constitutes the consumption–identity relationship, before beginning to reflect on why it is different today and how

this changes the ideological power and influence of consumer capitalism on our everyday lives.

The Psycho-social Self

At first glance it seems preposterous to claim that consumption has a
significant role to play in the construction of identities as compared to
manifestly more acute factors such as gender, race, sexuality and perhaps
even class. The fact that it seems so is precisely why we should treat such
a claim seriously. How and what we consume matters because we take
it for granted. Yes, of course, our gender, race or sexuality is a crucial
part of who we are. But so, potentially at least, is what we consume, not
merely because it represents a vehicle by which we express who we are,
but also because how we consume may feed back into how we feel about
ourselves. As Collareo noted in 2003, the sociology of the symbolic
and the communicative strategies employed in the construction of
self-meanings have long been a concern for social scientists. Indeed, the
way in which we consume arguably has as important a role in stabilising
our selves as communities and families used to (Knorr Cetina, 2001).
The role of consumption in identity construction has changed over
time. The ability to consume came to be more than just an economic
necessity, but a social and a cultural one too. It became a focal point for
how individualised consumers related to and felt belonging in a society
that came to be defined by the ability to choose and the freedoms that
this implied.

The concept of identity is a relatively recent one that did not exist
prior to the 1960s. Despite the complexity of the term it can actually be
defined in a quite straightforward fashion as, 'who we are and what we
know ourselves to be, whether that is in terms of our individual person-
alities and sense of self – roughly, "personal identity" – or in terms of
the social groups to which we are assigned an identity – roughly "social
identity"' (Moran, 2015: 12). It's of course important to remember that
identity is a highly contested concept. From one perspective identity
is primarily a psychological issue. Psychologists have long preferred to
focus on the notion of the self. Leary and Tangney (2012) identify five
different ways in which researchers commonly use the word self: self as
total person, self as personality, self as belief about oneself, self as exec-
utive agent and self as experiencing subject. But the point to be made at

this stage is that none of these notions of the self can exist independently of a social context. The self is a psycho-social construct. The experience society is sociologically important because it is psychologically important too. But what identity means now is not what it meant in the past: it is an old word used in new ways (Moran, 2015). Moran's argument is thus that identity today can only be fully understood if embedded in the cultural, political and economic contexts from which it emerges. What is important about the word identity then is not so much its changing meaning, but rather how that meaning has changed according to the word's relationship to the nature of social change. It is in this context that the relationship between consumption and identity in an experience society is worth further exploration.

I will come back to how Moran pinpoints the relationship between capitalism and identity later, but before I do so I want to consider a similar contention by Anthony Elliot (2016) that our contemporary life experiences have profound implications for both public and private identities. Elliot sees identity as a double-edged sword. The kinds of transformations we associate with a capitalist world that have multiplied our lifestyle options, not least through technological and digital innovation, have become associated with notions of freedom. And yet at one and the same time they appear threatening or intimidating: the risks we associate with late twentieth- and early twenty-first-century social change are arguably increasingly individualised. There is apparently more onus on the individual to navigate his or her own way through the uncertainties that social change brings. Moreover, it is Elliot's concern that at this time of technological revolution, serious questions about the nature of our shared identities and how they might be compromised in such a context has evaporated from public discourse as a direct result of a vogue for science and technology studies in the humanities. Elliot goes on to describe the complexities that the notion of identity takes on in a world of such apparent uncertainty. He thus refers to,

> the point that a world of intensive globalization, technological innovation and posthuman mutations thoroughly transforms the very meaning of identity ... the growing cultural anxiety which people increasingly experience today that their identity – their core sense of self, if you like – is rendered unfit for purpose in terms of confronting the core challenges and dilemmas of daily life. (Elliot, 2016: 3)

This is an existence characterised by anxiety (see Maguire Smith, 2008). In many respects modern existence is dominated by our relationship to anxiety, and the anxieties created by a culture that tells us we must work in order to belong, almost taking on a life of their own so that our self is a mirror to them (Elliot, 2016).

My concern in this chapter is how the nature of identity has arguably been recalibrated, transformed even, in the context of an experience society. Back in the mid-1990s the relevant discussion was about how identity was becoming increasingly privatised. The collectivities and support mechanisms that people could previously rely on were seen to be breaking down as part of a process of fragmentation that fundamentally undermined the ways in which identity was anchored. However, the irony of this process was that it propelled the individual towards the social, given that it obliged the individual to play out his or her self-preoccupations in public (Lodziak, 2002). Or, as Lasch (1984: 32–3) puts it, this process, 'freed the imagination from external constraints but exposed it more directly to the tyranny of inner compulsions and anxieties'. It is likely that in recent decades this process has intensified. We are all under increased pressure to transform and perhaps more importantly to be seen to transform. All conduct under these conditions is economic conduct; all spheres of existence are framed and measured by the economic and the crass commodification that this infers. Human beings thus effectively exist as 'market actors', desensitised 'to the bold contradiction between an allegedly free market economy and a state now wholly in service to and controlled by it' (Brown, 2015: 40). They are effectively the product of neoliberalism, an order of normative reason that determines every dimension of human life and which ensures that questions of identity are never resolved. In this kind of an environment Horkheimer and Adorno's (1972) suggestion that the consumer is forever on the cusp and never actually reaches the point of satisfaction is ever more pertinent. The challenges that tomorrow brings are so urgent that how we deal with the problem of identity today is only ever partial. Consumption is a coping mechanism but does not provide any kind of resolution. What Elliot (2016) is describing here is the individualisation of identity: a world in which individualisation is intensified but which does not necessarily bring with it increased individuality. The most important suggestion is that professional and personal reinvention has created a climate of what Elliot calls 'identity reengineering': a state of affairs in which the fashioning of do-it-yourself biographies has become paramount.

> In any case, the arts of reinvention practised through new individualism encompasses a great many experiences, ideas and ways of living. The current cultural fascination with instant change and endless self-transformation also raises questions about the social coordinates of identity in a world where long-term possibilities and sustainable futures seem fractured and brittle. (Elliot, 2015: 9)

Space, Consumption and the Evolution of Identity

However uncomfortable we might feel at the suggestion, many scholars have reflected on the extent to which the consumer is who or what he or she buys (e.g. Miles, 1998; Cutright et al., 2013). Such debates might range from a marketing perspective on whether what someone buys has a direct impact on how they perceive themselves, to a more sociological focus that might reflect upon whether an individual or group of individuals gains any sense of stability or belonging by associating him or herself with a particular style.

Some of the earlier contributors to debates around the relationship between consumption and identity such as Featherstone (1991) and Giddens (1991) have been criticised for apparently fetishising the stylisation of life and hence lifestyles to the extent that they arguably imply that aesthetic judgements are effectively taking the place of moral ones (Ray and Sayer, 1999b). For commentators like O'Neill (1999) such an approach is in danger of presenting a simplistic post-modern position which celebrates the frenetic fragmented nature of the individual who is apparently free to pick and choose an identity from one minute to the next. To adopt this position would imply that consumption is simply a matter of choice and freedom. It might suggest that the experience society is all about personal progress; the ability of the consumer to make the most of the opportunities a world of consumption provides. A core concern throughout *The Experience Society* is that the nature of the relationship between consumption and identity may well be changing and that *experiential* forms of consumption (as opposed to the consumption of objects per se) are much more pivotal in this regard than they may have been in the past. In other words that, in a rapidly changing world, the way in which what we consume contributes to who and what we are, and is arguably undergoing a noteworthy transition that has significant sociological implications.

The above transition is also, of course, very much a spatial phenomenon. It is a question of territoriality: the act of creating territories that are not neutral entities. Space plays a key role in how human beings have come to establish a sense of individuality and self-awareness (Sack, 1992). This process has taken hold over many centuries and is reflected by apparently innocent structural changes to our everyday existence such as the segmentation of rooms within the house, or indeed the invention of the mirror. In this context, Sack goes on to discuss the work of Yi-Fu Tuan (1982), who looks in turn at the development of the idea of self in relation to segmentation. In this sense, our experience of the consumer society is determined by our freedom and the burden upon us to create meaning. This reflects the emergence of a new regime in which value became measurable by money. Other processes such as the separation of home from work have led, according to Sack, to a state of affairs in which people, things and processes are not anchored to a place. Space has effectively taken on an abstract quality, and arguably that abstract quality is tied more than anything else to the economic needs of the consumer society. Most crucially of all,

> We need places of our own in which to build our own worlds … as the external world becomes more segmented, so too does the self. Territoriality provides the possibility of anchoring the personal sense of place to fixed locations in space. But because this personal sense of being in place is not shared – and because territorial partitioning may even reinforce its isolation – it's become private, subjective, and even idiosyncratic. (Sack, 1992: 5)

Thus, in a consumer society the thrust towards a new means of exploring a sense of individuality becomes relentless in its drive. Our culture obliges us to be intensely aware of our own selfhood and thus to have an inflated belief in a sense of our own individual power while seeking external recognition that it exists (Tuan, 1982). This is a long-term process in which the emergence of an experience society is the latest incarnation.

There may well be an argument for suggesting that cultural, social and economic change is such that appearance (as opposed to performance) is at least less significant in how we perceive each other than it was in the past: that there are signs that consumers are less drawn to objects as means of self-expression. Note, for example, the decline of the fashion market, not least among young consumers (Geoghegan, 2018). If we accept that this is the case, it may not take such a great leap of faith for us to begin to imagine that this may involve a reaffirmation of some of the principles of identity that authors such as O'Neill (1999) so value. In other words, we may, just possibly, be on the verge, perhaps in light of the current urgency of environmental fears about the future of our planet, of something of a return to a more positive age where character, skills and dispositions are at the heart of who and what we are. My point here is that consumer capitalism is sufficiently sophisticated to take such a transition, realistic or not, in its stride. Even when the individual feels the need to demonstrate his or own worth – even when he or she takes a step away from using consumer goods to this end – it will find a way. And experiences are the vehicle through which it is capable of doing so.

What we can perhaps contemplate is the suggestion that the process underpinning the construction of identity has gone full circle: a transition from a notion of identity that was communal or social in nature to one where human beings increasingly saw themselves as individuals independent of their social context and, in a sense, back again. At this point in history, in an age of individualised risk, uncertainty and dislocation, identity is arguably being redefined not least through social media, so that the way we perceive of ourselves is inevitably fragmented and yet personally intensified. Not only do we have less common biographies (and thus uncommon class positions) or cultures to call upon than we did in the past, the emergence of prosumption, namely a model of consumption in which the boundaries between consumption and production are diluted and in which the commodity is more commonly co-produced, accentuates the divisive nature of the world of consumption that frames our social world. The consumer is no longer the passive recipient of consumption, but plays an active role in determining what his or her consuming experience will be. From one point of view this is eminently liberating: in some respects the consumer has indeed become the author of his or her own consumer-based identity which at least feels like it offers a means of escape. He or she is freed up to make much more considered choices than even 20 years ago. But on the other hand, such a process ties the individual ever more directly to the very system from which he or she seeks refuge. As a result we become identity tourists, insofar as (despite the ambitions we might have for them) the pleasures of experience in which we indulge become nothing more than an end in themselves. We define ourselves not by who we are but through the nature of what we experience. In this sense the experience society is a fallacy. It is a society that robs us of the experiences to which we aspire beyond a momentary connection with that experience.

Selfhood Reinvented

In contrast to the prevailing theoretical wind that suggests that notions of identity may no longer be appropriate nor tenable, I want to argue that the sense of self that an individual constructs in an experience society is subtly different, and arguably more personally damaging than it was in the past. One of the key challenges of social and cultural theory lies in understanding what this change means for how the individual is defined through both his or her interaction with others and the mediating phenomena, such as consumption, that so profoundly inform such interaction (Holland, 1977). Holland (1977: 272) long ago argued for a radical science of the human, noting that 'any formative, social contextual influences operating on all theorists within the human sciences are located in self-concepts and include psychological variables. Thus it appears that the last thing we must do is leave psychology to the psychologists and sociology to the sociologists.' For Holland, the social sciences are distorted by their neglect for psycho-social mediations. Our insistence on seeing the act of consumption through disciplinary lenses must relent, as only then can we truly get to grips with the ideological implication of what I am describing here.

In his discussion of the relationship between consumption and identity, Dunn (2008) argues that it is the 'inscription of subjectivity' into the commodity that has led to a profound transformation in the nature of identity formation. This is perhaps primarily 'manufactured' around a perpetual sense of 'lack': the perennial feeling that something is missing. This is, in turn, representative of a process in which consumption is now less associated with social status and more with an intensification of the need for self-esteem. In this context, the notion of lifestyle remains key. For Dunn lifestyles are a vehicle for the construction of identity insofar as they provide resources through which the self can be defined, while also providing an outward expression of where the individual fits in a broader social and cultural context. Indeed, however individualised our experience of consumption might feel, it is still inevitably socially mediated. And yet this process appears to be less and less class related. In short, the commercialisation of identity politics and its focus on the array of choices and differences available to the individual have undermined the traditional structures that class provided, while the realm of consumption itself has widened the possibilities available to the individual well beyond the parameters that class used to provide. Lifestyle thus refers to either the ways in which a household chooses to spend its disposable income or to what such spending says about that household and its members' life practices. By implication, the notion of meaning is also particularly important. It is not what a person or a group consumes that matters but how and why. This helps us understand the emergence of the experience society insofar as it implies a changing set of circumstances in which the consumer is, or at least appears to be, increasingly empowered by his or her ability not only to make a choice but to act upon that choice in such a way that what he or she consumes becomes a highly personalised experience to the extent that life becomes 'an expressive vehicle of aesthetic intent' (Dunn, 2008: 125).

In this light, Helga Dittmar (2010) goes as far as to describe consumer culture as a 'cage within' because its unrealistic ideals lead many people to experience identity deficits and negative emotions, which they in turn go about solving by trying to construct a 'better' form of identity through the freedoms consumerism appears to provide. Far from providing an effective avenue through which we can construct sustainable identities, the argument here is that the symbolism that consumerism creates alienates us from our deeper psychological needs. Products are simply not equipped to give us what we subconsciously ask of them. Of course, there might be said to be a psychoanalytical dimension to all this, given Freud's (1920) notion that the guiding principle behind the functioning of human beings is the pleasure principle: the pursuit of pleasure and the avoidance of pain (see also Moccia et al., 2018). The concept of human drive is central to Freud's model, but for the purposes of this book it represents a diversion, the suggestion that human beings have an innate motivational drive being anathema to the psycho-social position I seek to present.

What is of more interest is the ability or otherwise of products to provide us with brief moments of satisfaction or pleasure, while ultimately achieving nothing more than a façade of ideal selfhood. The purchasing of designer brands is a useful case in point. We might believe that buying an expensive pair of Prada shoes will demonstrate to the world that we have a particular kind of elite taste and, perhaps more importantly, that we are able to afford to buy into the meanings that Prada implies. But such a strategy is counterproductive. Not only are the meanings we attach to such goods compromised by the diverse ways in which they can be potentially perceived by others (e.g. one individual's idea of good taste is another's 'crass consumerism'), but the power of their meaning inevitably and rapidly wears off. They could be the shoes we wear when we go dancing or our best 'dating' shoes. But in order for the self to feel that it belongs and in order for us to feel that we are in control of that sense of belonging they need to be more than mere shoes. The shoes are merely one element of a more impactful and less transitory experience.

The focus on the self is important here, but it may also exaggerate the compulsive and potentially anxious nature of consumption in the sense that you could argue that under the guise of experiential consumption such anxieties and compulsions are more effectively hidden. At this stage it is worth pointing out that what I'm discussing is part of a capitalist condition, indicated above, which perpetuates a state of affairs in which a meaningful and satisfying identity is never actually secured. As Lodziak puts it, 'whatever the attractions of consumerism, and our new found freedoms, they fail to satisfy what the individual needs to sustain a meaningful sense of self' (1995: 20). What is being described here is at least on the surface a never-ending cycle of dissatisfaction. From this point of view identities are plentiful and widely available, but at the same time the question of identity is far from satisfying or meaningfully resolved; they are transient and thus empty of permanent meaning. The suggestion is thus made that in his or her efforts to achieve identity stability the individual is drawn to superficial and transient associations. This has long been the role that consumption plays in providing a resource through which consumers feel that they belong. And yet what is actually being maintained here is something of an illusion of stability and of secure selfhood. Consumer capitalism maintains this state of affairs in order to maximise its economic 'benefits'. The escape into experience allows this to happen. In this makeover culture short-termism is prioritised given that long-term commitment and durable relationships appear to be less and less sustainable. This is a culture of excess, or as Elliot (2013: 91) puts it, 'in excess of itself'. The abiding question, however, is whether this is all an illusion: the way in which the self hedonistically deludes itself by cancelling out whatever it is that it cannot tolerate about itself. Can the consumer self-manage and what impact does experience have in this regard?

> Only through looking at past ways of doing things and previous forms of living or lives can we critically examine and better realize our dreams and projects. Reinvention is thus, among other things, always an engagement (however minimal) with the contours of invention. Yes, reinvention society may be shot through with the illusions of consumerism or celebrity culture, but still it holds out the promise of an engagement with the more positive currents of human creation … it is not a question of people having the wool pulled over their eyes, rather we are considering the narratives of reinvention people tell (themselves and others) in order to cope with and confront a world of advanced globalization. (Elliot, 2013: 93)

Commodities accentuate the kinds of tensions that social change brings (Sack, 1992). For the individual they provide a release, possibly even an escape, but for the capitalist machine they intensify the parameters within which consumers can be controlled. In Marxist terms experience feels like it shields the consumer from their alienation.

Identity and Capitalism

One of the most useful contributions to this debate, and one I would like to consider in more depth, is the work of Marie Moran (2015) in her book *Identity and Capitalism*. Moran draws attention to the fact that the notion of identity is both 'vital' and 'problematic'. In this regard a key concern has been the notion that in modernity identity is not simply pre-given or assumed; it is indeed performed. This is a notion that I will return to throughout this book. To put it another way, identity is a project: it is fluid and potentially fragile. Moran argues that the experience and expression of identity have become more prominent in recent years as a result of a realisation that having an identity is a universal component of what it actually means to be a human being. For Moran, 'The claim is not that people's "identities" came to matter more in late capitalism, but that capitalism itself came to operate as a new and key mechanism for constructing and experiencing a sense of self, and its relation to others' (2015: 4). To put this another way, capitalism and the subjectivisation (i.e. the constitution of individuals as subjective entities) it implies, work to create particular identities: capitalism has created a world in which human beings are both capable of and expected to possess an identity. And it is in this sense that the self is extended through consumption. We use possessions to enhance our sense of self. But the mere process of the self being extended by consumption only tells us half the story. Possession is no longer enough. The experience of simply owning a product is unacceptably transient. The consumer needs more.

The nature of identity has effectively shifted from one built on the solid foundations of work, employment and the market to one that has to be far more flexible and adaptable. Elliot thus describes a world which is simultaneously innovative and dangerous. The only way to adequately respond to the demands of this world, at least according to those that propagate it, such as politicians, personal trainers and business leaders, is to be personally flexible and constantly self-inventive, a process that has particular emotional implications for how we understand the body. In this context, Maguire Smith (2008) looks at fitness as an example of how capitalism teaches us to discipline as well as enjoy our bodies and how the body effectively operates as a status object, 'a site of investment and an instrument of self-production' (2008: 3). This is in part a class issue insofar as the middle classes have come to own this as a form of 'self-work', but increasingly, or so at least it seems, the sphere of leisure, as I will argue in Chapter 3, is available as a solution to the problems of the self and self as expressed *through* the body. Capitalism effectively tells us that what we do outside of work is there to help us make the most of our selves. Such a realisation has broader implications for our understanding of consumption:

Weaving individualization together with consumption, the problem of the self has, over the course of the twentieth century, become the problem of the consuming self, with the body as its project. Our bodies are reflected back to us through the lens of products and services, and consumption is promoted as the primary arena in which we are to make and remake our bodies. (Maguire Smith 2008: 20)

Maguire Smith argues that the world of self that consumption gives us access to is not one of self-production at all. We have no choice. The only choice is to become 'ourselves'. Fitness, from this point of view, is simply another form of work: and the pleasure we derive from it is one born of capitalist discipline. We have for too long had a misguided belief that personal style and personal advancement equate to individualism, and in turn to a notion of democratic equality. We are so invested in the cult of the self that we feel we have the right to anything we want (Hedges, 2009).

Flawed Consumption, Flawed Identities

Consumer capitalism encourages us to think that everything is available to everybody. Perhaps the best way to illustrate this point is not through the example of the consumer, but rather by reflecting on those that *aspire* to consume, but cannot, at least not to the levels to which they aspire. Bauman (1998) uses the term 'flawed consumer' to describe the way in which those who most aspire to the world that consumerism offers are effectively excluded. In effect, those who most feel the effect of the world of consumption are those who stand on the outside looking in, frustrated by the fact they are not able to be part of it. Bauman thus argues that our ability to consume, rather than whether or not we are employed, is now the defining characteristic of contemporary society. Consumers are 'flawed' in the sense that they are simply not equipped to participate fully in the society in which they live. They are socially degraded by their inability to consume and are thus left to feel bitter and shut off from the riches which appear to be available to everybody else (Bauman, 1998). So how does poverty feel under these circumstances? For Bauman, the consumer society professes a world in which boredom is impossible and yet uppermost in people's minds. Those who are bored only have themselves to blame in a consumer society. They have failed. They do not belong. Our society obliges us to belong; so we have to experience what that society offers. The point here is that this process magnifies the role that consumption plays in how people see them-selves. The irony is that the more someone is excluded from the world of consumption, the more they arguably define themselves through what it is they cannot have or what they can only experience by overextending their debt and thus tying themselves ever closer to the economic regime that defines them.

'Flawed consumers' do everything in their power to use the symbolic power of consumption in order to demonstrate their belonging, and indeed power. This can certainly be said to have been predominately acted out in the past through the consumption of products and in par-ticular fashion, as Newell (2012) demonstrates in her work on crime, consumption and citizenship in the Ivory Coast. Newell describes the way in which young unemployed men in the Ivory Coast use brand names in a very deliberate fashion as a means of asserting their social authority. For these young men, or *bluffeurs*, such consumption indi-cates a sense of pride. They are deemed successful, they have a degree of authority because they are seen to be so. This is consumption as perfor-mance; the use of products to create an experience or a set of conditions in which the experience of being a consumer becomes real and very vocal, even if it was acquired illegally and arguably inauthentically.

These young men have no legitimacy other than that they present through what it is they consume. And that is actually all they need. Everybody knows that these young men are poor, but they are able to use their consumption to assert their own sense of authenticity which is mirrored in the eyes of their audience. The authenticity of consumption is established *through* performance. At an ideological level this is further evidence of the seductive powers of consumption both for the consumer and for those consuming that performance. However, the 'authentic-ity' of the *bluffeurs* is not unique or indeed vaguely unusual. There are echoes here of Paul Willis' (1978) classic work on working-class school boys, *Learning to Labour*, in which boys conspire to reassert their own downfall by asserting themselves through status-bearing behaviours that ultimately tie them to a future of exclusion and possibly work-lessness. Again, this exclusion isn't the production of consumption or production per se, but rather a means of representing some semblance of authenticity to the outside world. Or to put that another way, a pre-sentation of self, where the self is protected by a veneer of power and authority. However, this power and authority inevitably slips through the fingers of a real world that is relentlessly unforgiving and which will ultimately judge you on the basis of your misguided efforts to belong.

Consumption has always been performative in one way or another, as the example of the *bluffeurs* demonstrates. In a sense, their example is not dissimilar to how the youth cultures of the latter half of the twentieth century used consumption to their own ends. In both cases the value of fashion lies in its symbolism: in what it tells others about group membership and belonging. But perhaps the difference here is that the performance is built on divergent grounds. The stylistic choices of punks, skinheads, rockers and the like provided visual indicators of a class position (see Hebdige, 1989). For the *bluffeurs* the performance and the experience of the performance is everything. Yes, wearing particular brands offers them status. But above all it mitigates and legitimises their flawed consumption. By being seen to be consumers they 'belong' *as consumers*. But such a feeling is ultimately an illusory one.

In seeking to understand the positive impact of experiences on people's lives we might well come to the conclusion that experiences have the potential to make us happier than investing in possessions (which ultimately become props to our experiences). The reason for this is that experiences are more open to positive reinterpretations, and thus from this point of view have the potential to contribute positively to our social relationships (Van Bowen and Gilovich, 2003). The other side of this is that experiences may not distort our sense of self in the way that possessions do. For example, our society is ridden with social norms and expectations around what constitutes beauty, fashion and the like, and these set the standard for how people are expected to behave and look. A good example here, somewhat perplexingly as far as this author is concerned, is the common or garden eyebrow. The fashion for how you are expected to present your eyebrows as a young woman is a matter of fashion that constantly changes, and may vary according to your age and your geographical location. Similarly, there are significant pressures on young women to wear make-up in particular ways that appears to have very little to do with aesthetics; what matters here is the performance and the experience of that performance. Just because the majority are wearing heavy make-up, for example, doesn't mean that the young woman concerned is presenting herself to the best effect. Rather she is conforming to the standards defined by her social setting and the demands on her to perform in prescribed ways. It is in this way that the consumption of physical things such as make-up help us feel that we belong, but simultaneously constrain the parameters within which we are able to do so. Lukes' (2005) discussion of 'internalised illusions' reiterates this point. Human beings do not construct their identities according to a personal and free choice, however much consumerism might imply this is possible. Their sense of being is inevitably tied up by a set of social processes which serve to mislead them and their judgement in such a way that their sense of self will always be compromised. We believe that by 'owning' our eyebrows as indicators of belonging we become masters of our own destinies; that we have control. But the opposite is true. By committing to the make-up regime that such eyebrows imply we commit only to perform our experience. We may feel better for it but something is lost in the process.

Conclusion

The social psychologist Helga Dittmar (2010), whom I have already referred to briefly, calls for a research agenda that looks at simultaneities of uniqueness: how it is that consumers fit in through what it is they are seen to consume, and how this offers uniqueness while simultaneously denying it. It is in a similar context that McGowan (2016) discusses the psychic costs of the emphasis on consumers as market actors. McGowan argues that capitalism dominates because it mimics the structure of our desire while hiding the trauma that the system inflicts upon us:

> Capitalism commands accumulation and promises a satisfaction it cannot deliver. This failure has its origins in the structure of the subject's psyche and the way that the subject finds satisfaction. The psyche satisfies itself through the failure to realise its desire, and capitalism allows the subject to perpetuate this failure, all the while believing in the idea that it pursues success. (2016: 21).

For McGowan (2016), being a consumer is about the experience of never finding satisfaction, but relentlessly pursuing it through the signification that consumption generates so that the repetition of loss that this involves brings its own satisfaction. This is an interesting way to pinpoint what the experience society is all about. Experience gives us the tools to maximise our personal 'journeys' and yet it perpetually teases us. It leaves us on the cusp and never actually brings us to a point when we have arrived. As I noted above, this process was long ago identified by Horkheimer and Adorno (1972), but it has changed radically. The existence of a so-called experience society is testament to the fact that this needs to be recognised. How we consume is a much more refined and personal matter than it was in the past. We not only see ourselves through how others see us based on what we consume, but we see ourselves *through* experience, regardless of how that experience complements or detracts from the wider social context in which we operate. The ideological impact of consumer capitalism is thus extended by a move away from the momentary consumption of products towards the more intensive and extended process of consuming a number of products and services, experientially.

All forms of consumption are quintessentially ideological. Because we accept consumption in all its magical guises as being normal and mundane its power intensifies. We 'live' capitalism through its commodities (see Fiske, 1989). The intensification of selfhood has gradually opened up the doors to a world in which such privacy has come to be represented by the world of prosperity and ease that the consumer society implies – a world 'without constraints and without responsibility' (1989: 199). The consumer is pulled into this world of escapism. In Tuan's (1998) words, we are thus more and more encouraged to escape from the animal state of our own existence. For Tuan, everyday life is in fact about unreality – it's uncertainty and lack of definition create a sense of the unreal to the extent that we aspire to something different to a world of simplicity and pre-established ritual, of consistency and self-discovery, a world in which we can be alive outside the problems that the world provides for us and in which our sense of who we are is magnified. The potential problem with this is that escapism is all well and good, as long as it offers a temporary respite, but if taken too literally it can become its own hell-like existence. Reality is what we decide it *has* to be. This takes us back again to the imaginative power of consumption and its apparent ability to provide the balm we need to get through, and indeed outside of, our everyday lives (Campbell, 1987). What is interesting about all this is the way in which the world of consumption portrays itself as a world free from constraint and the obligations that characterise everyday life, to the extent that our actions as consumers feel as though they are without consequence. Ironically, we seek escape in order to belong, but belonging can never feel like we imagined it would (see Sack, 1992).

The experience society propagates the myth that now that products have failed us (or have themselves been reinvented as experiences) we can turn to experiences of whatever description instead, as a means of propping up our sense of self. Experiences provide the primary means by which we can proactively assert our own sense of self-worth and belonging; it is the basis for self-work. The experience society convinces us of our ability to control, however trivially, the world that surrounds us. We have constructed our very own *Truman Show* where all that matters is us. For this reason consumer capitalism is more powerful than it has ever been. In the kind of self-oriented environment it reproduces – in an environment in which the consumption of material things cannot achieve what it is we want – experience appears to offer a valid alternative; a more meaningful way of meeting our personal identity needs. The more we feel 'ourselves' through what we experience, the less control we have over the forces that make us feel this way. Experiences are thus more mouldable to the individual's identity than a consumer product per se, in the sense that they more easily offer the possibility of added value to our lives. They provide a conduit through which what is and isn't significant to us can be played out.

The contention that I will consider throughout the remainder of this book is that the consumption of experience perpetuates and intensifies the above process. I will thus go on to reflect what it means to consume leisure, sport, café culture, architecture, technology and work, and how this might inform our understanding of how and why capitalism reinvented itself. We might assume that an apparent shift away from products and towards experiences might detract from the so-called cult of the self that Hedges (2009) describes: that experiences are necessarily, or at least usually, more social in their orientation and thus less self-centred than an individual's apparently inward-looking relationship with a particular item of clothing, for example. But the reality is that a world that focuses more and more on experience puts the individual at the heart of his or her perception so that how he or she engages with that society is increasingly the product of how he or she imagines him or herself through the mirror that those experiences provide.

3

Leisure and Tourism

The leisure society does not exit. And it never did. Indeed, the technologically driven world in which we live appears no nearer to securing
the utopian ideal of a leisure society. And yet, leisure continues to evolve
in ways that appear to infatuate the consumer. The worlds of leisure
and tourism that we engage in are both very similar and yet different
to those we would have experienced just 30 years ago. Consumption is
the driving force behind this to the extent that how we spend our leisure
time is filtered through how and what we consume. But whereas leisure
used to be a means in itself, that is, an escape and a relief from work,
it is now a means to an end: the end being the proactive propagation
of self. The leisure and tourism in which we engage represents a form
of 'self-work': a form of work that reinforces the ideological power of
contemporary capitalism and which leaves us less in control of who we
are than ever before. It is through leisure and tourism that the personal
benefits and rewards of a leisure life are most tangible, and yet at one
and the same time they are demonstrative of the power of consumer
capitalism to take us to a place where we are most easily moulded into
the consumers it needs us to be.

The Leisure Society and the 'Escape' from Capitalism

Many authors have sought to understand the evolution of leisure through
capitalism. Rojek (2010) thus considers the status of the so-called leisure
society thesis which he describes as being intimately tied up with the
proposition that the affluent society expands the range of choices available to consumers while markedly improving the range of choices and
freedoms that they can access. This is the thesis that the world is getting
better and that it is capitalism that is making that happen.

As early as 1967, the French sociologist Dumazedier presented a
socialistic vision of leisure and asked whether it was emerging as the

new opiate of the people. His conclusion was that leisure was central to an emerging social life, that working people did have more time at their disposal and that leisure, in effect, constituted a 'mediating factor' that 'lies between the general culture and the totality of his activity' (1967: 231). For Dumazedier a society where leisure has emerged as a key institution offered hope of a more creative and self-fulfilling world: a world that promised to challenge the world of misery, ignorance and fear that preceded it so that, crucially, work had effectively become a means to an end rather than an end itself.

But were such visions overly optimistic? Could leisure really deliver the kind of balanced social existence to which such authors aspired? Perhaps the leisure society thesis found its most important, if indirect proponents through debates around the post-industrial society in which authors such as Touraine (1974), Bell (1973) and Toffler (1981) argued that technology was emerging as a means of liberation. They claimed implicitly, and highly questionably, that the growth of leisure was demonstrative of social progress and human emancipation (Rojek, 2010). However extreme such views might appear to us today, leisure has certainly climbed up the sociological agenda; by the last 20 years of the twentieth century it had become acceptable for sociologists to argue that leisure (and by implication consumption) was more than a simple by-product of work and production. However, as Rojek (2010) also points out, it was all too temptingly easy to exaggerate the universality of the leisure age. Yes, the consumer society expanded our choices, but it certainly did not revolutionise how we related to a society that continued to define us largely through how we work. To say leisure is more prominent than in the past is one thing, to argue that it is now at the heart of how human beings experience the world is quite another. An author considerably less optimistic in this regard is Jeremy Seabrook (1988), who describes leisure in the industrial era as something that is precious and insufficient. He ruminates about why it is that our culture holds on so tightly to a future vision of a society more leisured than our actual experience:

> Crossing the desert of the present (which is, after all, where we live) requires vast enterprises devoted to escape. What is it that so many of us feel such a pressing need to escape? It certainly cannot be that we suffer a surfeit of reality for we already live in the most escapist

society the world has ever known. It may well be that the need for escape is the wish to avoid an absence of significant activity, a lack of function and purpose: it is a way of mourning the loss of those very things which we are constantly being urged to greet as the source of our liberation. (1988: 4)

This tension has long been characteristic of our relationship to capitalism: a desire to escape from its demands, apparently counter-balanced by the irony that such an escape is almost inevitably itself forged in capitalism's guise. Perhaps this sense that we can escape has been made more tangible than it has ever been before by the possibilities that experiential consumption opens up. It's important nonetheless to recognise that this is something quite different from and yet related to broader notions of individualisation and the sense that at the end of the twenty-first century social bonds are breaking down. As I suggested in Chapter 1, social change towards the end of the twentieth century was such that the kinds of social institutions that gave us a sense of security and belonging in the past were undoubtedly beginning to decline. The role of community and religion, the latter clearly still significant but fragmented, are cases in point. Human beings were gradually being freed up to be who they wanted to be, but there was a price to be paid for this: a world of anxiety and uncertainty in which a person's travails were no longer dissipated but fell on his or her shoulders alone (see Beck, 1992).

One of the most significant examples of work that has sought to understand how, in recent decades, social structures have actually been disintegrated is that of Robert Putnam (2000), who argues that although the rise of electronic communication and entertainment has been personally enlightening it has also created an increasingly privatised and passive form of leisure so that we spend more and more time consuming goods and services *individually*. Such trends have no doubt been intensified since the publication of Putnam's book, not least in light of the rise of social media. What has certainly changed is the way in which we invest meaning in what we consume, and what we ask of it. I pointed out in Chapter 2 that social change was resulting in what is an intensification of the feeling of selfhood. This intensification reflects a state of affairs in which, as Garcia (2018: 5) puts it, 'Modern society no longer promises individuals another life, the glory of what lies beyond, but rather promises what we already are – more and better.' It is not enough in our society to simply get through the day, we must be seen to live, love, work and play to the absolute maximum. The point is that such intensity is measured by ourselves: we are the judges of our own ability to be ourselves to the extreme. And the irony of this of course is that as we all go about the everyday business of experiencing everything 'to the max', if everything becomes intense then nothing is (Garcia, 2018). Intensity becomes the new norm, and the soulless beneficiary of this is a consumer capitalism intent on convincing us that our need to feel as much of ourselves as possible can be met by the market:

> If the modern mind demanded novelty, it was mostly for this reason: the body and mind are a blazing chalice fuelled by intensity; all the while, old intensities pass from the embers of the unknown to the ashes of the already-identified. The world loses its charge of intensity unless we constantly recharge it … The spectacle and consumption of intensities … were crystallised in the promise of the entertainment industry, nickelodeon, movies and theme parks. Everywhere you look, there are different products that attempt to convince the working public to part with their money in exchange for feeling alive. (Garcia, 2018: 68–84)

The more we seek intensity the more we weaken our ability to experience it; but more importantly, the more consumer capitalism is able to thrive. If we were to chart the history of how consumer society has evolved we might well recognise not only that society has become increasingly simulated, as authors such as Baudrillard (1991) have suggested, but that such simulation is apparently being readily embraced by more and more consumers. Such developments are the product of a society intent on maximising the experience of selfhood for purposes of economic sustainability.

Leisure as Personalised Experience: The Theme Park

A good example of leisure as personalised experience is the theme park. For Gottdiener (2001), themed environments constitute extensions of the kinds of social forms critically analysed by members of the Frankfurt School; they are 'regulated places of consumer communion' (2001: 172): staging grounds for social interaction and for the enactment of capitalist intent. The extent to which such spaces can be used by consumers in order to achieve self-fulfilment, given that themed environments are arguably designed to incorporate any such counterhegemonic tendencies, is certainly a matter for debate. What is clear is that how consumers interact with commercial spaces cannot be solely a personal thing. It is inevitably the by-product of a process of social reproduction that taps into the very fantasies that in turn serve to maintain consumers' commitment to the everyday world that they escape from and reinforce at one and the same time.

The theme park is perhaps the ultimate expression of this process. It is a space for idealised consumption and escapism in which the togetherness of escape is the order of the day (Jensen, 1999). Such spaces are often described as carefully controlling what it is that the consumer can consume in a space that leaves the contradictions of the outside world behind (Lukas, 2008). But it doesn't leave that world behind at all. Yes, in one sense, theme parks play a socially therapeutic role: a way to forget yesterday and tomorrow, a 'new temporal and spatial order' in which the consumer can live the moment to his or her maximum effect. But what is particularly interesting about Lukas' analysis is the suggestion that the theme park actually offers more than this: it is designed to change people's lives, and with it *their souls*. By providing a full-on escape, spaces such as the theme park convince us of our freedoms, but in the process tie us ever more closely to the world from which we seek to escape.

In the above sense the theme park doesn't provide an escape at all, but rather an extreme model demonstrating how it is we should live. We tend to think of theme parks and specifically the fantasy narratives that they provide as existing *outside* the real world. But of course, theme parks largely define that world *through* forms of consumption. How it is we understand our sense of self and our connections to others is, among other things, a product of the brands, symbols and associations that a theme park perpetuates. Like consumption more generally, the theme park doesn't reflect or provide an alternative reality, it reproduces that reality. It is no less than a stamp of approval of a way of life. In effect, the theme park has evolved to construct new forms of sociality and self–other relationships (Lukas, 2008), but it does do through the filter of capitalism, thereby reinforcing powerful notions of the whole and our place in it:

In a theme park, and perhaps only in a theme park, people can once again have a feeling of being connected. As one moves from one ride to the next, into a restaurant and then into a gift shop, and even a restroom, one can feel that the whole is whole again: everything is connected to everything else through the marvel of theming ... Even though rides tell different stories and shops sell different products, the approach within any given theme park space is to control through the *one* perspective, the branded, corporate and optimistic one. Just as religions limit the space of narrative interpretation, the theme park form allows for a limited and powerful discourse about the world. (Lukas, 2008: 242)

Unsurprisingly, Davis (1997), who looks at the production and consumption of the theme park *Sea World* in Southern California, describes the archetypal leisure spaces of the theme park as a money-making machine, a machine that provides the consumer with access to a rich cacophony of culture on the surface, but which is in fact deeply uniform in its delivery and content. What is more interesting here is the way in which places like Sea World make consumers *feel*. The experience of consumption has in this way gradually been reinvented, so that it is far from the simple using up and laying to waste of products implied by attendance at an event, experiencing that event and then moving on. The act of visiting Sea World is, as Davis (1997) points out, in actual fact presented to the consumer in an apolitical guise; as a means by which the consumer can act upon their concerns for nature while participating in the common good. From this point of view just being there is a form of 'doing', but the work that is being done here is the work of capitalism. Capitalism commodifies nature: it presents it to the consumer as something to be consumed just like any other commodity. By doing so it changes our relationship to nature, while intensifying consumer capitalism's ability to determine our existence. Capitalism commodifies nature, to the extent that the theme park becomes a primary and indeed a supposedly 'natural' means of experiencing it. As a touristic form of nature, Sea World presents a kind of indisputable wholeness that 'takes part in a rationalized process of extraction: it extracts profits from the labor of its workers and its animals, from the manipulation of its landscape, and from the desires of its customers' (Davis, 1997: 243). But Sea World is far from alone. A weekend away with the family at a Center

Parcs holiday village does exactly the same thing: it effectively themes nature and in doing so ties its consumption into broader notions of class status (Miles, 2016).

Capitalism manipulates the consumer into engaging with nature in a particular way and our experience intensifies that process insofar as it gives that process an air of individualised reward. It makes it feel more real, in the sense that the individual is made to feel that they 'own' it. Herein lies the irony of the experience society. The more we feel we experience the world of our making, the more we feel self-vindicated, and the more we tie ourselves to a world where the control over who and what we are is diminished.

Tourism and the Manipulation of the 'Authentic' Self

A brief discussion of the theme park hints at the potential power that experiential forms of consumption have to reinvent how it is that capitalism is perpetually reproduced. But it is much more omnipresent than such an example implies. Tourism is the arena in which such manipulation is perhaps most readily felt insofar as it is the arena through which we, or at least those who can afford it, most readily seek escape from the demands of everyday life. McCannell (1989) draws attention to the way in which the contemporary tourist seeks authenticity as a kind of contemporary pilgrim. He or she looks to embrace experiences outside his or her everyday life so that everything he or she confronts becomes something to be consumed. In this context, staged authenticity becomes the norm. This is an idea that Urry (1990) develops further with his discussion of the tourist gaze. Tourism generates pleasurable experiences that we appreciate or at least anticipate in particular ways: it creates demand for them where demand did not previously exist. There is a significant element here of fantasy and daydreaming; of intense pleasure seeking (Campbell, 1987) and most of all a sense that the experience must be extraordinary: 'potential objects of the tourist gaze must be different in some way or another. They must be out of the ordinary. People must experience particularly distinct pleasures which involve different senses or are on a different scale from those encountered in everyday life' (Urry, 1990: 11–12).

You could argue that there is nothing new about this: that tourism has always been experiential in some shape or form. But my contention is that something has changed: the aspirations that we may have previously channelled through tourism now percolate across our experience of consumerism as a way of life (Miles, 1998). More radically, I want to suggest that although today's world of leisure and tourism may not be transformative in the way that some theorists of the leisure society may have suggested, and that although our access to leisure isn't markedly greater than it was in the past, what leisure we do have access to has more of a role to play in 'self-work': the way in which consumers use consumption to actively contribute to a sense of who they are and how it is they relate to the uncertain economic world around them (Brown, 2015).

Tourism is all about producing a particular kind of value for the consumer and that value does not lie in some inherent quality of a product or a location, but in our experience of it and how we compute its effect, to the extent that authenticity isn't inherent in a place but is determined by the individual's sense of self and how they choose to define their interaction with a place or an experience. For many then tourism is a profoundly psychological process (Quinlan Cutler and Carmichael, 2010). In one sense tourism is, of course, about the creation of memories which are inevitably deeply subjective, and they thus have to be the product of how the individual engages with and views a tourist experience in retrospect. The tourist experience is constituted in a combination of novelty and familiarity, and involves an individual's pursuit of identity and self-realisation (Selstad, 2007). Thus, many authors have suggested that escapism lies at the heart of an 'authentic' tourism experience. This may be constituted in the form of an escape from the mundane demands of the everyday, but also, by implication, from the pressures imposed upon us by the society in which we live. But the key question here, as Cohen (2010) notes, is how far such an escape is possible and whether it is inevitably socially constructed, or indeed as Rojek (1994) puts it, can only actually amount to a projection of the dominant values of the society in which we live. From this point of view, any notion of escape is utterly forlorn (Rojek, 1994).

Tourism as Performance

Perhaps a useful way of exploring how leisure and tourism has been transformed in recent decades is through the lens of performance. In this context Cohen (2010) quotes Butler's (2008) work on performativity and points out that identity construction is an embodied performance that is processual, to the extent that the individual is always 'on the stage' and 'within the terms of the performance'. Performances are ways of doing 'identity'; or as Bell (2008) puts it, ways of doing aspects of identity such as sexuality, gender, ethnicity and age are performative insofar as they are negotiated through a process of 'becoming'. There may be some forms of tourism (see e.g. Cohen's (2010) discussion of 'lifestyle travellers') that lend themselves more explicitly to aspects of 'authentic' identity construction than others, and in doing so appear to support the notion at least on the part of the travellers themselves that they have a 'true self' to aspire to. The more general point, however, is that in an experience society questions of identity, however partial and performative, become more urgent and more consistently part of the everyday. The self may not be integrated in the way it was in the past, but that doesn't make it feel any less urgent in the moment. In fact, in an uncertain, fragmented world it becomes a core element of our everyday experience. Performance is the norm to the extent that, as Jones (2019) puts it, tourists have become as keen to see themselves in the city as they are to see the city itself. The need to construct the self in an experience society has become normalised, thus more easily serving the imperatives of consumer capitalism.

As we speak I find myself in the privileged position of sitting in a chapel in the grounds of a mansion house on a personal 'writing retreat'. When explaining to friends and family where I was going for my retreat I referred to this place as 'a chapel in an enchanted forest'. My experience of being here has been very much bound up with my anticipation of it. Of course, the forest isn't enchanted. I constructed this version of events to serve my own purposes. The accommodation itself is relatively basic. Its value lies in how I have gone about experiencing it: as a place in which my authorial self will be realised, where I will write the enchanted words fitting the setting of 'my' enchanted forest. It is in this notion of the particularity of experience that tourism produces a particular set of values (see McCannell, 1989; Sternberg, 1999). What is interesting about this for our purposes is McCannell's contention that products aren't simply products, but that they constitute a means to an experiential end: that 'the end is an immense accumulation of reflexive experiences which synthesize fiction and reality into a vast symbolism, a modern word'

(1989: 23). But what if, over time, the nature of these reflexive experiences had been intensified? What if the balance between the role of the product (e.g. the hotel, or in my case this perfectly formed yet freezing chapel) and its interpretation, or our ability to believe we have free rein to experience such a product as we see fit, has been recalibrated? Does this open up space for a more persuasive consumer capitalism?

Modern culture is characterised by the room it provides for the individual to make his or her own assessment of the commercial reality that lies behind the cultural experience that they are offered (McCannell, 1989). The process of cultural production does not simply deposit models or versions of social life to be consumed. Cultural experiences are, in fact, lived expressions of societal values, and perhaps most importantly of underpinning economic ones. McCannell uses the example of the professional footballer whose actual value is not established until it is played out as a form of cultural production to be consumed. This is manifested today in the Premier League and in a world in which top players can be paid as much as £300,000 a week. Such astronomical sums are possible because the magic of the Premier League generates its own form of enchantment to be consumed.

For example, a fan of professional football in England a hundred years ago may have simply consumed the match-day experience. Such an experience would have been much more localised than today. The players would often have been recruited locally, while matches would have been primarily the focus of the local print media. But gradually this changed, and soon professional football found its home on television. By the 1980s *Match of the Day* was a regular fixture on TV in the UK, and the FA Cup Final had long been shown live every year. Football was very much a matter for national consumption. However, by the 2010s the landscape was very different again. The Premier League and the Champions League catapulted professional football into an entirely new realm of profit making. As a result, the way we experience it is a world away from its origins. It has become a tourist product. It has become routine for supporters from other countries to travel to Britain to watch Premier League matches. But more than that, the consumption of football, thanks to the internet and to social media, is constant (see Chapter 7).

In one sense, how we consume football has become more distant. You do not have to be a local person to support a club or to know the fine detail of what's happened in the latest transfer window. Football is global, but it has also become a different kind of experience, one that is apparently more of a personal choice and one that can take many more forms than in the past (e.g. going to the match, creating your own fantasy football team, managing your team in a computer game, tweeting about the abilities or otherwise of your manager, following the tweets of your centre forward, calling into sports radio and contributing to national debate about the team). The experience is potentially less immediate and yet more immediate at one and the same time. What it isn't is any more real or authentic than it was in the past. In fact you could argue it is markedly less so. What is different is that it *feels* more immediate. Football has been 'leisured' so that we each consume it through our own lens. The intensity this implies only partially hides the fact that what we consume is much more fundamentally filtered by a media intent on maximising profit for the game. As McCannell (1989) would perhaps put it, nowadays football promises a greater quantity and quality of experience. His argument, albeit back in the 1980s, was that this process effectively turned the worker against 'himself' in that he is thus obliged to construct his own synthesis between work and culture, and that it is only in such a synthesis that some semblance of humanity can be found. This notion that we are somehow searching for our own humanity is an interesting one. The conundrum here is that the more we seek that sense of humanity, the more we are dependent on the very entity, namely consumer capitalism, that takes it from us.

Consuming the Spectacular

If Premier League football is anything it is a spectacle. One way that leisure persuades us of its ability to change us is through the process of spectacularisation: by giving us access to spectacular experiences that appear to offer something entirely different to our everyday lives. Two authors who have looked at this question particularly effectively are Krier and Swart (2016), whom I mentioned in Chapter 1. In developing Debord's (1995) notion of the spectacle, Krier and Swart argue that our experience of the social world has come to be defined by a series of flickering images and representations that distract us from everyday life. Their contention is that there is a high price to be paid for the world of spectacular consumption which has come to characterise the everyday. In effect, capitalism has come to destroy the nature of collective consciousness. The way in which we communicate and generate relationships has, from this point of view, been superseded by new modes of communication and indirect relationships that we now pursue through leisure and consumption. The point here is that spectacle 'provided an illusion of social life while in fact enforcing deep estrangement of self from other' (Krier and Swart, 2016: 21). It's in this way that leisure presents itself as a kind of perennial carnival; a way of life, but one that is in fact nothing more than a stage for the marketing of capitalism through the construction of self (see Jensen, 1999). Such forms of tourism are, from this point of view, empty diversions; emotionally distant experiences through which the power of capitalism is long forgotten and yet increasingly intense and urgent.

The particular argument that Krier and Swart go on to present is that spectacular rallies and motorsports in the US such as Sturgis and NASCAR are inherently self-negating insofar as they are reproduced as commercially exploitable commodities, which in turn undermines their intended status as cultural forms. Krier and Swart argue that far from constituting spaces where choices of marketised enjoyment are liberating, spectacles such as Sturgis and NASCAR deanimate their essentially passive participants. Their thesis is that the actual experience of such events is much more disconnected than it may appear on the surface, so that attendees are often more distracted by the hunt for souvenirs representing their experience than they are in enjoying the experience itself, to the extent that 'Pleasure is derived not from the moment of the trophy's purchase, but from the realization of surplus enjoyment in another place and time' (Krier and Swart, 2016: 131). You could argue that such an interpretation undercuts any kind of a notion that we live in an experience society insofar as what we might imagine to be the peak moment of experiential engagement is in fact more of a means to an end. But the point here is precisely that our conspicuous relationship to such events *is* experiential. We may feel bored and listless during such an experience, but we reassure ourselves that what we are experiencing is meaningful and in the process our alienation as vehicles for the propagation of consumer capitalism is redoubled by the ways in which we justify the benefit of the experience to ourselves (Krier and Swart, 2016). Having a good time is not sufficient: the consumer needs to *prove* it, and experiences are the means by which they do so. In effect, experiences are the pseudo-individualised products of our time (see Horkheimer and Adorno, 1972).

Cruising and the Democratisation of Leisure

Another example of what could be argued to be a spectacular (and yet in some ways mundane) form of experiential consumption is cruising. Cruise ship tourism has become incredibly popular in recent years. At one level cruising is a straightforward example of consumption as status aspiration. Traditionally the public image of cruising has been about the consumption of luxury. And certainly, 30 years ago, the public perception of cruising was of a form of leisure that was available only to those who had the appropriate economic capital. Cruising was an expensive and exclusive enterprise, one that most of us could only dream about. But over the years cruising has been, or at least appears to have been, democratised. Cruises are arguably nowadays less about the consumption of luxury by the privileged classes and more about an opportunity for consumers of all backgrounds to taste the 'high life' in its various experiential forms (Kolberg, 2016), such as partying cruises centred around bands and dance, boutique cruises aimed at the more discerning consumer or even cruises deliberately designed to feel as un-cruiselike as possible. Meanwhile, a whole tranche of companies designed to appeal to the budget cruiser such as Celebrity Cruises or Thomson Cruises have materialised. But what's changed here is more than just who it is that is able to partake in the consuming experience. Yes, capitalism has predictably found a way to adapt its offer in such a way as to expand the market, but in the process it has also reinvented what it means to consume.

The appeal of the cruise ship lies in its ability to take passengers from place to place in a very time-efficient fashion (see Miles, 2019). And yet, at one and the same time the nature of the experience of these places is necessarily diluted. From this point of view the cruise ship is a socially constructed built environment that serves as a 'container for commodified human interaction' (2019: 5). Such spaces work insofar as they sell an experience, and in doing so a fulfilment of an emotional need on the part of the consumer (Goulding, 1999). The possibility of self-work is realised through the canvas that the cruise ship provides. The cruise ship thus becomes an idealised space for experiential consumption as opposed to simply a place for the demonstration of status through consumption. What I am suggesting here is that the popularity of cruising may constitute another indication of a transition towards consumers self-consciously engaging with what they consume in a more experiential, but also a more psycho-socially proactive, fashion. In effect, the consumer feels 'total involvement with life' (Csikzentmihalyi, 2002; Mitrasinovic, 2006). On a cruise ship anything *feels* possible. What the cruiser might be said to cling to on a cruise ship is a partial and temporary form of self-discovery, a kind of personal peacefulness that could and will be taken away at any minute, but one which is nonetheless highly anticipated before the event, and quite possibly a matter for regret afterwards. In this sense the pleasures that these forms of experience provide come, as I suggested above, at a cost. This feeling of intense selfhood is in danger of being offset by a longer-lasting sense of loss and uncertainty. It's this tension that intensifies the consumer's pursuit of fulfilment. He or she may not feel satisfied or self-realised by a cruise, but the prospect that he or she may be never goes away.

The cruise ship is thus indicative of a broader trend towards self-authored tourism (or a form of tourism that at least suggests the freedom that this implies) in which the consumer becomes the 'subject' or the 'product' of his or her own consumption, insofar as the cruise experience allows him or her to construct a consumer-driven version of themselves through the setting the cruise ship provides. Such an experience serves to perpetuate the consumer's need to find a form of self-actualisation that consumption cannot actually, ultimately, be relied upon to produce. In fact, more than that its very success depends on its inability *not* to provide such satisfaction (McGowan, 2016). It is for this reason that the cruise ship passenger, and indeed the consumer more generally, keeps coming back for more: in the expectation that it will be better next time. The individual is thus both actor and audience in his or her own drama, 'his or her own' in the sense that he or she 'constructed it, stars in it, and constitutes the sum of the audience' (Campbell, 1987: 78), so that the individual has increased responsibility for the ideological demise in which he or she finds him or herself. The consumer effectively experiences being someone else, or at least feels like they can be someone else through the escape that the experience offers. But the cruise ship performs luxurious escapism in such a way that while it offers self-discovery on the one hand, on the other hand it takes it away, by closely defining the routes through which self-discovery can be achieved and making their actual achievement an impossibility. We define ourselves not by who we are but through the nature of what it is we experience. And herein lies an indication of where the world of consumption may be going and the role that tourism may play in its maintenance.

Airbnb and Self-authored Tourism

A key question of concern underpinning my discussion in this chapter appears to be the extent to which consumers can genuinely escape via forms of experiential consumption. However, of equal import here is the way in which forms of consumption are constructed so as to convince us precisely that we can. The rise of Airbnb as a tourism phenomenon is a clear expression of this process. Airbnb constitutes one of the most significant changes in how consumers engage with the world of tourism, notably through the way in which the company has created an omnipresent and credible alternative to the hotel that, from a marketing point of view, explicitly focuses on the ability of the consumer to design their own experience. There is a sense of what authors such as Ritzer and Jurgenson (2010) have described as 'prosumption' here: the consumer takes responsibility for the choreography of his or her experience. While acknowledging that production and consumption have never operated fully independently, Ritzer and Jurgenson (2010) argue that this reflects a longer-term historical trend (see also Tapscott and Williams, 2006) in which business has increasingly put consumers to work, whether it be pumping petrol at the filling station, scanning one's own food at the supermarket or playing a part in the performance and reproduction of a themed space, such as Disney. The Airbnb consumer is much more in control of his or her tourism experience than a hotel guest would have been in the past.

Not only is there considerable online work involved in choosing an Airbnb 'home' – in ways that may not be the same if you were simply seeking the most convenient hotel, given that the sheer extent of choice puts a burden on the consumer to choose wisely – but he or she is also obliged to replenish the production process by rating the experience. The most successful Airbnb hosts present their homes as their guest's own and they present it as an experience for the consumer to construct to his or her own ends, thereby indicating that this isn't just about the liberation of the consumer, but about the emergence of a much more sophisticated collaborative form of production. So, for example, an Airbnb resident will often receive a 'welcome pack' which provides all the practical information they need to know about their stay and the opportunities that are available to them. Through this mechanism the home becomes a stage set for self-work. My own experience of Airbnb included one property in which the owner provided a printed lined drawing of the property alongside a set of crayons, the expectation being that as the compliant guest, I would colour in the drawing and pin it up alongside those pictures dutifully provided by previous guests: a visual demonstration of a maximised experience. Sure enough I did, for not to do so would betray my vision of myself getting the most out of my precious time for escape.

All this is not solely about the transition of accommodation from a function to a need, nor is it simply about building possibilities for memories that will bode well when it comes to the guest reviewing the property online. It is also about engulfing the guest in a metaphorical warm blanket of experiential belonging. It is about giving the consumer props which they can use to author their own experience and to take away with them a sense of how they are developing in light of fulfilling such opportunities. As Brian Chesky, co-founder and CEO of Airbnb, puts it, 'These are deep, insider immersions into somebody's world … We think this is a totally unique vertical that doesn't exist today … Right now travel is oriented around being an outsider, having limited access to public places … This is about being an insider and immersing in a community. And that is a profound shift' (Gallagher, 2017: 193–4). Not only does it seems unlikely that an immersion of this kind is even possible in such a short space of time, the point here is that such an immersion may feel like it is has *become* our world, when the reality is it is simply nothing more than a distraction from it. Moreover, as a business Airbnb has been subject to something of a backlash, with many cities fighting against the sheer pressure of numbers caused by 'tourism pollution' and the suggestion that Airbnb is destroying not only the hotel sector, but also that of accommodation rental (McCurry, 2018). Airbnb may be changing consumers but it also changes places in the process.

Some of the processes I am describing here are undoubtedly tied up to what Gallagher (2017) describes as a general decline of human connection and a growing separation of society in which we are increasingly persuaded into a more solitary kind of existence. This is in turn intensified by a feeling of unease in a world that constantly reminds us that we have no control: a world where the threat of terrorism is apparently immediate; a world in which we feel we need to belong and look to find new ways by which we can do so: what Beck (1992) called a risk society. But as I suggested above, it is doubtful whether Airbnb can actually deliver such a connection. Perhaps consumers are more willing to engage in less conventional, more quirky and thought-provoking forms of tourism than they may have been in the past. But even if they are, there seems to be quite a heavy price to pay: in such circumstances, the consumer isn't exploited through the obligation to produce this experience, but ironically through the sense of agency that the experience apparently facilitates. However, this is not, ideologically speaking, a one-way street. It actually raises many concerns that sit in contrast to Rifkin's (2014) argument that the shift towards prosumption constitutes 'an eclipse of capitalism' as a result of which old economic paradigms are breaking down. If the consumer engages with his or her experiences in such a way that his or her sense of self is enhanced or simply altered as a result, the potential ability of consumer capitalism to control the consumer while ensuring that he or she is tempted into commodifiable relationships with the material world, is surely increased dramatically. Not only is the means for the consumer's self-exploration intensified by the transition towards experiential consumption, but so is the ability of consumer capitalism to exploit this process in order to maximise profit along the way.

Conclusion

Dunn (2008) points out that what it means to consume is increasingly suffused with notions of pleasure and experience. It is of course not the case that consumers did not previously find consumption to be pleasurable, but that the experience of pleasure and its role in how we perceive our sense of self is arguably a more pivotal element of the consumption experience than it was in the past. Sternberg (1999) thus describes the process by which the ability to present oneself has become a valuable economic (and cultural) asset, to the extent that the individual is obliged to position him or herself and the pleasures they attain through consumption, in respect to their audience:

> Now in the fabulous era, the new economic man is epitomized by the celebrity cosmetic surgeon. Through self-presentations that build his own celebrity, he not only profits himself but prescribes the facelift and antidepressants that also serve society, palliating fear, restoring confidence, and making patients feel good in their anxious rush to produce persona for the market. (Sternberg, 1993: 82)

This, I want to suggest, is very much tied up with the increased responsibility that the consumer has for the management of his or her own consumption. This brings us back to Gottdiener's (2001) point that the contemporary consumer is engaged in the consumer society through body *and* mind. One example of this is fitness, which I also raised in Chapter 2. It is no longer enough to go for a jog around the block to work off our Christmas excesses. We need to be seen and to feel that we have subjected ourselves to a fitness regime that defines who we are. The pressures on young men to maintain the body perfect is a case in point. Time spent at the gym is no longer part of a lifestyle; it is a life; it defines us. How we consume becomes who we are in an arguably more profound way than it was in the past. Accepting as much leads us to a point where the power of leisure and tourism as vehicles for the maintenance and reproduction of capitalism needs to be reconsidered. The contemporary consumer desires the entertainment and fun that consumption can offer them, and is willing to put in the groundwork to help achieve that, but in such a way that directly plays into who or what they are, and perhaps more important how they feel. As far as we can identify a historical shift here, it is a shift in the meaning of leisure and tourism away from a place being consumed and towards the person consuming a version of themselves that they would not otherwise be able to access, but for the anonymity that such places provide. As Tuan (1982: 7) puts it,

> daily life, with its messy details and frustrating lack of definition and completion – its many inconclusive moves and projects twisting and turning as in a fitful dream – that is unreal. Real, by contrast, is the well-told story, the clear image, the well-defined architectural space, the sacred ritual, all of which give a heightened sense of self – a feeling of aliveness.

Our conclusion might be that what this all this adds up to is an opportunity for the well-educated, enlightened person who has lost trust in authority to make independent choices (Jensen, 1999). That what we are witnessing here is effectively a liberation of the individual, so that the consumer is no longer dependent upon their social setting or standing: 'The emancipation from the fixed menu has a clear corollary: it has become absolutely necessary to make an independent, individual choice' (Jensen: 108). But individualism is not all it is cracked up to be. The liberation it produces inevitably results in anxiety, self-doubt and uncertainty: exactly the kind of anxiety, self-doubt and uncertainty we might have imagined individualism was supposed to offset. Our consumer experiences provide us with a measure of contentment, insofar as they transgress our everyday norms, and we see them through rose-tinted glasses (Wallman, 2013). But they also bring with them infinite pressures and personalised dilemmas. The stories that consumerism provides us with are more compelling, more immersive, more 'real' than they have ever been: we are where we travel. If we can afford to travel, that is. We are the product of our own intensities; the product of a constant balancing act that goes on between the ups and downs of everyday life and how we interpret that in order to impose on ourselves a sense of our own identity. We live a life of intensity, but such intensity is ultimately empty in that it can never provide the promise that appears to underpin it, and a life of exhaustion is the end product (see Garcia, 2018). The experience society perpetuates this process and as such, as Horkheimer and Adorno (1972) would no doubt have put it, the consumer is indeed forced to be satisfied with the menu.

The experience society operationalises an unheralded degree of ideological control at a point in history in which leisure and tourism have paradoxically and ironically become less about the individual than they have ever been. As long as leisure and tourism provide us with an escape, as long as they provide us with a means of finding and feeling 'our selves' through the stories that have effectively been constructed for us, as long as this continues and as long as it can be redesigned and reinvented through new guises and experiences, the further away from where we thought we were travelling we will go and the more powerful consumer capitalism will become.

4

Work Experience

The experience society is characterised by the opportunities it appears to provide for human beings to take ownership of the moment; to be the masters and mistresses of their destinies; to take control. In this chapter I want to reflect on work as perhaps the most pure bastion of experience. Can work really provide us with the sense of fulfilment and satisfaction that consumption cannot? Or is work in fact subject to the very same processes of commodification? What can the world of work tell us about the ability of capitalism to reinvent the world in such a way that we feel that we are maximising our personal impact upon it? In this chapter I will consider the suggestion that what might be described as the 'experiential consumption' of work is effectively a mirage; a mirage of self-fulfilment in which a sense of self is rarely won and most often lost.

Work and Social Change

In a sense, work is a sociological minefield. It has long been a core component in how the individual relates to society and vice versa. But what is most interesting about work is perhaps its ability to conceal the true nature of that relationship. It's in this vein that Foley (2011) describes work as something of a religion. He argues that whereas we used to work to live, now the reverse is true. For him any kind of a notion of a leisure society is laughable. Work is everything. But what work is more than anything else is a fulcrum for the power relations that underpin the society in which we live.

In some respects the apparent centrality of work in our lives is bewildering. We deride the experience of work as a matter of course: that's what workers do. There's nothing we like to do more than complain to our fellow workers about how bad things are, and yet at the same time we crave the relatedness that work can give us. We relate to it, perhaps subconsciously, as the vehicle through which we can find our selves.

The power relations that characterise the workplace are far from subtle (Weeks, 2011), and because of and perhaps despite those relations, it is apparently normal to value the experience of work deeply, or at least be seen to do so, as though it says something very important for and about us. Work gives us a sound footing in a world that is otherwise changing around us, and by doing so it convinces us that we, as individuals, retain some semblance of control:

> The workplace, like the household, is typically figured as a private space, as the product of a series of individual contracts rather than a social structure, the province of need and individual choice rather than the site for the exercise of political power ... As a result of work's subordination to property rights, its reification, and its individualization, thinking about work as a social system – even with its arguably more tenuous private status – strangely becomes as difficult as it is for many to conceive marriage and the family in structural terms. (Weeks, 2011: 4)

Herein lies the power work has over our lives. Work integrates us. It defines us as citizens and as breadwinners that have earned the right to belong. And yet, our union with work, a union that is encapsulated in our desire to succeed as individuals, is actually attached to *paid* work which is arguably less about individual or social wealth and more about the private appropriation of surplus value (Weeks, 2011). Work defines our ability to belong, or it at least competes with consumption as a primary means of doing so (see Bauman, 1998). Bauman talks about how it was that work used to be a lifelong driving force for the construction of identity and how the workplace operated as the primary site for social integration. However, in a consumer-driven society the work ethic is apparently superseded by the aesthetic of consumption. The consequence of this is effectively a trade-off between our dependence on the consumption of products in order to satisfy our desires and the fact that this implies greater dependency on our employers to provide us with a working wage (Cremin, 2011). For Bauman, being poor is no longer defined by unemployment but by the ability, or otherwise, to consume, or to experience, consumption. As I suggested in Chapter 2, the 'flawed consumer' is defined by the frustration inherent in the relentless obligation to feel and indeed demonstrate a sense of belonging without being equipped with the resources that allow him or her do so. Under these circumstances, as work becomes less important, it becomes more so, in the sense that it becomes a form of psychologised consumption. To put this another way, our experience of work is as a commodity that demonstrates the extent to which we can meet the demands of a consumer society. Work becomes another means of asserting our sense of belonging, and we live it, experience it, squeeze what we can out of it, because we are privileged enough to be able to do so and because it props up our sense of self in a society where what we present ourselves as becomes who we are. And yet the more we seek the refuge that work might provide, the less we can apparently secure the individuality which we so crave.

Sociological Approaches to Work

The relationship between work and consumption has long been a key sociological concern. John Ransome (2005) argues that the general shift from a work-based social type to that which is more consumption based means that an individual's social position and social orientation is nowadays much more the product of a broader notion of identity and thus less singularly dependant on occupation. What is interesting about this shift is the contention that the limits on how we understand individuality are much less fixed in the case of consumption than they would have been in the past in the case of work. What this means is that although work remains an important element of who and what a person is, it has a less exclusive status in this regard. But perhaps more pertinent here is the contention that how workers actually see work has changed, so that there is arguably now a greater emphasis on work as a potentially autonomous and pleasurable realm. From this point of view there has been a shift towards work as an arena in which the self can seek a degree of satisfaction (Ransome, 1999). Ransome thus considers the suggestion that although many jobs are of course inherently non-creative, the ambience of our work experience, our determination to find work that is genuinely 'me', may be more and more on our minds, thereby creating a situation in which the boundaries between work and non-work are also shifting. This reflects the emergence of a new individualism in which the self has become the new object of late modernity (see Chapter 2): a state of affairs that isn't simply about consumption replacing work as the primary sense of identity, but more about the emphasis on the former reinforcing our commitment to the latter.

Work ties us to the society in which we live and it also represents a measure of how that society is changing. The point here is that the development of that society goes hand in hand with the individual's commitment to it through his or her recognition that it allows him or her to be. Weeks (2011) reflects on Weber's (2002) contribution to our understanding of the experience of work, and in doing so suggests that work is increasingly crucial in how it is the individual delays gratification and invests in self-discipline in order to maintain and protect his or her own self-development. In effect, '"Life" with its wealth of possibilities is subordinated to the disciplinary demands of work' (Weeks, 2011: 48). Weber (2002), of course, recognises that the work ethic is an individualising force, or at the very least we feel that it is. It is because we see it that way that it provides the basis for our exploitation, as well as broader elements of inequality (see Weeks, 2011). More than that, you could argue that such a process promotes the docility of work. The notion that work could ever be an experiential domain further intensifies this suspicion. Such a notion convinces us that work is of our own making and that we can, after all, construct the very best version of ourselves through the mirror to our selves that work provides. Yet, in fact, what we are arguably doing here is losing ourselves to the predictabilities and conformities that work demands of us, so that the self to which we aspire is further and further from our grasp. Our relationship with work is therefore highly disconcerting, discombobulating even. Work arguably provides us (or at least some of us) with more and more opportunities to be creative and to engage with our work in a way that assimilates our emotional intelligence. But by buying into this we are dependent on a system that in turn depends upon the loss of our self, and thus manufactures a state of affairs in which the worker is ideally suited to reproduce the capitalist system (Weeks, 2011).

Perhaps the author who has managed to most effectively understand the impact of the changing nature of work on the self is Richard Sennett, who as early as 1998 argued that the conditions of time in contemporary capitalism, and specifically the risks and uncertainties it creates, results in a conflict between character and experience. For Sennett, uncertainty is woven into the everyday experience of capitalism. For him the shift that has gone on here is one that used to be about the delayed gratification of the work ethic and yet which became increasingly self-destructive, insofar as self-imposed discipline was superseded by an ephemeral world characterised by constant change. The impossible challenge for the individual thus lies in his or her lack of opportunity to gain power over him or herself, when that self is constantly subject to the uncertainties of capitalist reinvention. From this perspective, as a result of our dependence on a winner-takes-all market mentality, the experience of failure becomes ever more common regardless of your class. In such a state of affairs, it is easier to construct narratives around the past than it is the future. For this reason our experience of work is all about living in the moment; a moment couched in our collective (and often negative) memories of the past. In what Beck (1992) refers to as 'the second modernity', this tendency to live a 'life of one's own' and thus the compulsion to construct an 'individualized horizon of meaning' (1992: 53) becomes increasingly profound as part of a deep-rooted historical change in which human beings have become authors of their own lives. Of course, this brings with it considerable uncertainties, and perhaps it is in the workplace that these are felt most acutely. This is partly a systemic change in which the relationship between organisations and individuals has been eroded by the short-term insecurity of employment contracts and the threat of social and economic polarisation that this brings with it.

Beck (2000) takes up the above theme further in charting the inherent ambiguity of the new world of work that's being described here and the fact that such freedoms come with a price. He argues that the traditional world of work in which a person could pursue a lifelong path is a thing of the past and is being replaced by a world of instability, skill devaluation and welfare degradation; a world of risk biographies. The issue here is perhaps that the status of work in people's lives has sky-rocketed so that it has become 'the core value and mode of integration' (Beck, 2000: 11) in modern societies. Central to this transition, as I pointed out above, is the individualisation of work: the shift away from work's standardisation that has primarily been stimulated by technological change and the placeless interactivity of networks. The practical implication of this has been a more 'flexible' kind of work experience. We might expect some aspects of this to be positive: many forms of work have apparently benefited from more flexible working policies that give the employee more say over when and often where he or she works, and would thus be assumed to promote a more satisfactory work–life balance. However, the reality is not quite as clear as such an assumption might suggest.

There is indeed evidence to say that by individualising the work experience such practices actually have the effect of intensifying the pressures of work: grateful to have more freedom, the compliant employee often works even harder in the new, so-called flexible arrangements. This is often about employees feeling that they have to work harder in order to offset the dangers of job insecurity (Kelliher and Anderson, 2010). As Tietze and Musson (2010) argue, working at home can create conditions in which the worker can benefit from a work experience capable of contributing to a stable sense of self. Work may or may not be as demeaning or exploitative in the past (Pettinger, 2016). The increase in part-time work and in more flexible arrangements such as working at home or flexi-time may or may be, to an extent, liberating. But what we do know for certain is that such changes in the experience of work do not exist in a cultural vacuum. Rather they are embedded in wider social relations in which both consumption and the consuming self are deeply implicated to the extent that human beings are arguably as commodified as workers as they are as consumers (Pettinger, 2016). Such freedoms are mostly class specific and have the potential to disrupt as much as to stabilise.

But what does this all have to do with experience, and more specifically the rise of an experience society? Consider what it means to work, as I do, in a university. University lecturers are surely among the most fortuitous of workers, not least given their apparent freedoms and the latitude they have within which they can self-manage; not to mention the space they have to explore their academic passions. Academia perhaps then provides the ultimate experiential employment insofar as it offers the latitude the academic needs to be what he or she wants to be. But it is not always as simple as that. Academics are a disgruntled and permanently infuriated bunch. Their assessment of their own work experience is often non-reflexive and vocal, musing on their lack of time, the excessive hours they commit to the job and a sense that this cycle of despair is never ending. Such a sense of anguish is intriguingly individualised, as if no one else experiences such demands in the same way that they do. The default position is one of bureaucratic incredulity, and this is a profession that many would reason is comparatively well paid and high up on the scale of creative endeavours. But what academics experience, as do many other professionals, is a kind of individualised helplessness, and it's this helplessness that sits at the heart of Sennett's (1998) analysis: 'This is the problem of character in modern capitalism. There is history, but no shared narrative of difficulty, and so no shared fate. Under these conditions, character corrodes; the question "Who needs me?" has no immediate answer' (1998: 147). In a sense the problem is perhaps not so much the reality of the experience of work, but the perception of it in a bureaucratic context in which it is easy to conclude that the individual is entirely lost. Capitalism is indifferent to its workforce. The soft power of the market has an increasingly incendiary impact insofar as the contemporary worker is obliged to learn how to bear instability and fragmentation; the experience of work is thus individualised, although not always in the kind of positive ways we might imagine (Tweedle, 2013).

The desire for more fulfilling work only serves to reinforce this state of affairs. Indeed, any sense of satisfaction with work is inevitably a momentary one: one in which we convince ourselves that we have been able to forge a path in which we could be our true selves. This chapter has inevitably led myself to reflect on my own personal experience of work. I have recently found myself pretty much as happy and content with my career as I imagine I could be. And yet ironically, for fear of destabilising the status quo, part of me has been conscious not to be seen to be outwardly happy in the workplace. For to do so would be to offend the habitus of that workplace and to threaten my own position in it. The worker is disposable. And of course, it has always been this way with capitalism. But what has changed is that it has all become more personal (Sennett, 1998). The intangibility of our work experience is such that it is increasingly hard for us to envisage our own sense of belonging. The workplace experience might feel less oppressive, but that's because its oppressiveness has evolved into something much more subtle. However free we are to manage ourselves and our own time, we no longer know where we stand or whether or not we are needed. We are entirely subject to the slings and arrows of outrageous fortune. Better, or more decent work, is simply an experiential cloak that protects us from the salvo of uncertainty that characterises our everyday working lives.

The New Workplace

Perhaps the most obvious way in which work has changed, at least in some quarters, is architecturally, or perhaps ergonomically. In a sense, capitalism or its propagators have come to realise the economic benefits to be had in facilitating the worker's sense of well-being. There are, of course, many examples of workplaces that deliberately emphasise the potential of the individual experience. To this end, Borges et al. (2013) discuss the history of workspace design and argue that an empowering psychological component has been gradually built into the contemporary job description. This could be argued to have built upon a Fordist modernity in which efficiency was the key characteristic of a workplace symbolised by the factory. The increasing significance of the office and later of the service economy intensified the feeling of alienation and malaise until the onset of a more post-Fordist age in which jobs became more ephemeral. What materialised was a new guard of businesses that chose to put the onus on providing the conditions under which their workforce could 'think out of the box'. Indeed,

> The transformation of a work experience into a social experience – where co-workers become a second family and the office itself a home away from home – operates as a strategic tool on the part of employers to reframe how we feel about our jobs … Understanding the frustration that can arise when employees feel cut off from their personal lives, the new office landscape cleverly adapts itself to fill these psychological and social voids. (Borges et al., 2013: 4)

The emphasis of such spaces is said to be on creativity and on individualised freedom: on providing a space in which the employee can better balance the divide between what they do and what it is they want to do and be. To this end, Borges et al. wax lyrical about the liberating benefits of workspace design in companies such as Facebook which has worked hard to blur the boundaries between work and play: employees being, for example, encouraged to add art work and write on walls in a way that mirrors their online patterns of behaviour. These are stimulating experiential places; adult playgrounds in which the human imagination is apparently unconfined. Similarly, Google's London headquarters provides a kind of collective living room in which workers are encouraged to develop meaningful relationships with their co-workers: what is being offered here is a stage set in which work and home coalesce (Borges et al., 2013). But the concern here is that when you have a scenario in which the individualisation of work and the individualisation of life more generally coincide, society is itself in danger of falling apart (Beck, 2000). Superficial changes in how we experience work might tell us something significant about the darker side of social change more generally. To this end, Beck (2000) quotes Castells (1996) who presciently points out that, 'Under the conditions of the network society, capital is globally coordinated, labour is individualized. The struggle between diverse capitalists and miscellaneous working classes is subsumed into the more fundamental opposition between the bare logic of capital flows and the cultural values of human experience' (1996: 476).

The network society thus constitutes a new mode of development in which the capitalist mode of production has been restructured around informationalism. In this context the relationship between production, experience and power is reformulated. For Castells, production is about appropriating and consuming nature for their own economic and social ends; experience is about human beings being in a perpetual quest for the fulfilment of needs and desires, while power is the product of how production and experience relate so that the will of some subjects are imposed at the expense of others, either violently, physically or symbolically. Castells sees experience slightly differently to how I understand it, in the sense that he focuses on it being centred around how men dominate women in a network society. What is of particular interest for our purposes, however, is Castells' suggestion that what characterises this new age is 'the action of knowledge upon knowledge itself as the main source of productivity' (Castells, 1996: 17). The result of this emphasis on knowledge and indeed the power of technology to produce knowledge (see Chapter 5) is, according to Castells, its diffusion through all social behaviour, constituting what are in effect new forms of network-driven social interaction and social change.

As far as work is concerned, what all this means is that over time the worker has been empowered through technology (e.g. through automation) to produce more efficiency and flexibility, so that the conditions which underpin work are decentralised (e.g. through subcontracting, outsourcing and customising) while the experience of work itself becomes increasingly individualised. But of course the price to pay for what appears to be a more dynamic labour force is one that is actually more vulnerable and less secure. A network society is innovative and timeless: the generation of capital and value is immensely flexible and centred around a meta-network of financial flows, 'where all capital is equalized in the commodified democracy of profit-making' (Castells, 1996: 503). You could argue that in the terms of this book, the individualism and the intensification of experience that comes with it is entirely illusory and constitutes nothing more than a means of maximising profit while fragmenting, segmenting and disconnecting human beings from each other in the process. While capital thrives in hyperspace, the collective identity of labour dissipates forgotten under the cloud of personal professional development.

This brings us back to Chapter 3, in which I raised the apparently unrealisable prospect of a leisure society. Beck (2000) contemplates the danger that new working conditions might create a deep class-based fissure between the active and the passive. What makes leisure leisure is the fact that it exists for its own sake. But how far is this really the case? Is leisure, and the experience society leisure implies, any kind of an escape at all? If work no longer exists as we used to understand it (as regular secure paid employment) how can the experiences that the experience society provide for us be valid? How far do they provide access to our real selves?

Perhaps the best way to proceed is to consider work as a place of consumption as opposed to one of production. This is an idea that is explored in Sennett's (2006: 137) work in which he argues that a consuming passion is a passion that 'burns itself out by its own intensity ... Here the imagination is strongest in anticipation, grows even weaker through use' (2006: 137). For Sennett, work plays a key role in shifting this consuming passion from something that is essentially passive (e.g. as a recipient of fashion or of planned obsolescence) to something that is more proactive. Work is characterised by constant change and a jockeying on the part of the individual. This is a process of constant bureaucratic ingenuity that is mirrored by the reinvention of the individual that it creates. Flexible organisations increasingly require increasingly flexible skill sets, thereby creating an atmosphere of individual achievement and self-consuming mastery. Sennett thus describes a broader state of affairs in which branding and potency become absolutely essential. Branding becomes the object; it obscures homogeneity, magnifying minor differences in such a way that the surface becomes everything. The digital world, in particular, has encouraged a situation in which the individual 'curates' selfhood. The individual effectively invests in online relationships, cynically perhaps, in order to secure a professional reputational benefit (Gandini, 2015). In this way the self is itself a commodity. But what is important here is that stimulation doesn't lie in the consumption of the product, but rather in the opportunity to move from one product to another (Sennett, 1998). We consume work just like we did, say, the Sony Walkman in the 1980s. It provides us with access to a magical world of possibility, the next tape we put in the machine promising to be the one that makes our sense of happiness complete. It could be argued that the consumer has effectively come to realise that he or she need not only be satisfied with the menu (Horkheimer and Adorno, 1972): that he or she needs something. But the irony is that however much the individual tries and in whichever arena of his or her life he or she tries, ultimate frustration is the result:

> Marx's dictum 'all that is solid melts into air' was balanced, in the opening pages of Kapital, by a quite different analysis of commodity fetishism. To Marx, mundane things invested so magically with human meanings dwelt in a kind of personal museum, one in which the consumer added more and more to his collection; the consumer hoarded his treasures, his aim was accumulation. The last thing the consumer wanted was to give up these fetishes into which he had invested so much of himself. Now ... surrender of an object is not experienced as loss. Rather abandonment fits into the process of finding new stimulation – the objects particularly easy to give up since they are basically standardized goods. (Sennett, 2006: 150)

Work is the new stimulant that the worker needed. But such a need wouldn't have come about but for the broader demise of the object. Sennett (2006) uses the example of the iPod (itself already hopelessly obsolete) in demonstrating how it is our relationship to objects that has changed. The appeal of the iPod lay in its ability to offer the consumer access to more music than they could ever possibly need. In this way, the iPod was a potent product and this potency massively expanded the consumer's potential capabilities and experience in a way that could not even have been imagined at the time of the Walkman. Of more interest here is the suggestion that the iPod is essentially sold to us as an empty product. What technology does in this instance is compel us to pseudo-individualise the iPod through downloadable content (Cremin, 2011). The consumer is aroused by the endless personalised possibilities implied by the machine and its ability to set us free from the routines and constraints of everyday life. For Sennett then, contemporary consumption is all about theatre: objects evolved to offer the consumer desires and capabilities that are capable of not just buttressing a sense of self, but of actually stretching the boundaries according to which the self operates. Work becomes a focal point for this way of thinking. It becomes a form of consumption itself. A form of self-consumption, in fact, in which work is less about meeting organisational goals and more about exceeding personal ones. Work is no longer about maintaining an equilibrium, it is about being stimulated and finding something out about ourselves in the process. Of course, the extent to which this is the case is inevitably dependent upon the kind of job a person has and the extent to which it allows the individual room for manoeuvre. The ability to choose in this regard is not universal. Just like any other experience, that of work is a matter of class, education and privilege.

The Future of Work

Before I reflect more on what all this means for our understanding of the experience of work, I want to look in a little more depth into the notion that I began to consider above that the future of work is being revolutionised. One way of understanding the world of work is as being fragmented; fragmentation bringing along with it isolation, exclusion and narcissism. The problem with fragmentation, according to Gratton (2014), is that it undermines the ability of the worker and the workplace to shift from shallow generalism to serial mastery. The key thing here is the role of play in work and the fact that in an increasingly intense and pressurised working environment the opportunity to blur the lines between work and play, so crucial for the freedom and creativity of work, is potentially eroded (Gratton, 2014). As I suggested above, this process is intensified by technological innovations that may appear to simplify tasks, but which also have the potential to fragment our lives, not least through the demands created by a constantly networked world. Gratton sums this up by describing the transition from the voracious consumer to the impassioned producer. From this point of view the humanity of work depends on our ability to create a balance between the individualised self-focus of work and our ability to maintain genuine and strong working networks that are not all about the self.

The construction of self through work is not an isolated project. In exploring the notion that work is a modern religion, Foley (2011) contemplates the fact that the work experience is in fact built on an unholy payoff between the surrender of freedom, the façade of unrelenting care and the satisfaction of needs that the workplace provides. The world of work that Foley describes is a self-contained village built on the foundations of social networking. And in part the experience of work is so important to our lives because it provides us with a canvas, a cocoon perhaps, within which a certain kind of liberated self can be cultivated. But the problem here is the self that we construct for ourselves in the workplace is simplified: one often created for the consumption of our colleagues. As Foley (2011: 168) puts it, 'The problem is the loss of identity involved in surrender to the group – the mask has fused into the face'. Indeed, in the workplace we hide our true feelings: by finding ourselves in the workplace we simultaneously lose it. Yes, we are networked; but such networks are pathological. They are often partial in nature and tie us to others working as equally as hard as ourselves, more likely persuading us that we are not working hard enough.

Even those initiatives that purport to prioritise well-being and mental health are founded upon an organisation's commitment to the quantification of their employees, so the more that organisation responds to those needs, the less individual their employees can be. The concern here is that the contemporary workplace has reached new levels of control in this regard. As Moore (2018) suggests, the contemporary workplace not only seeks to quantify and hence control the body and the mind in the name of workplace agility, it effectively seeks to do the same with the workers' experience of emotions so that ultimately the personalised nature of work is indeed intensified, but only in such a way that the anxieties of precarity come closer and closer to the surface.

Gratton talks about the freedoms to choose that are created by new forms of work. Such places provide the worker with the opportunity to create kinds of social capital that may make our working lives feel less precarious. For him things aren't perhaps as bad as they seem. He argues that success and competition are no longer as influential in our working lives as they were in the past and that work is increasingly implicated by more inclusive forms of social capital. In a world in which earning money and achieving status become less important as a means of validation, the individual is freer to experience in a less constrained fashion, through friendship and mentoring for example, so that money is just one element of a broader gambit of the experience of work in which the self gives as well as receives: 'In the traditional deal it is ... purchases that have defined who we are in the society in which we live. But as the future-proofed deal emerges, it is possible that our work will be defined less by what we consume, and more by the experiences we produce' (Gratton, 2014: 311).

The emphasis here on the production of work experiences rather than their consumption is an important one. The temptation is to foresee a future in which the worker is liberated not only in the conditions which support the act of work (the opportunity to take a break to play a game of ping-pong or to give oneself some thinking time on a colourful arrangement of futuristic sofas, for example) but in the actual doing of the task itself, so that the individual is less constrained by the tight parameters within which his or her allocated tasks reside. Gratton (2014) argues that this kind of a world is achievable if we can get to a point where we think more deeply about work so that restraint becomes the priority and work becomes more purposeful as a result. This is an attractive prospect, but one that does not sufficiently take into account the broader ideological contexts in which the shifts she describes are taking place. In part, the problem is that the word experience inevitably implies a kind of freedom to choose, a locus of control, and can never be played out in the way that we as individuals and as consumers might imagine. In short, such freedoms are illusory. The freedom to enjoy what appears to be a more balanced and fulfilling working life is fraught with compromise. Capitalism is in the process of reinventing work not because it frees up the worker, but because it allows him or her to feel they can be free. The more we seek a balanced work experience, the more our self is at the heart of how we see the workplace and the more we are destined to be mere playthings of the experience society.

The impact of work as experience on our lives is potentially profound. Social change is seductive. Ransome (1999) thus criticises the work of MacCannell (1999) and other theorists concerned with the rapidity of social change for overexaggerating the extent to which production is becoming *less* exploitative. Specifically, Ransome's concern is that theoretical whim and fashion came to see work as a form of 'masquerade' and self-expression that said more about the determination of theory to prove a post-modern point than it did about how the real world of work was actually changing (Ransome, 1999). The point here, as Ransome (1999: 242) suggests, is that although there might well be some kind of amorphous generic sense in which work has become more flexible, such flexibility is actually provided on the whole by the worker who makes themselves more available and willing to work hours they wouldn't have worked in the past. Inevitably, the need for the job to be done is far more significant than who does it. The worker is disposable. The future of work is therefore likely to remain one of alienation. Of course, as I have already acknowledged, there are such things as creative, fulfilling and rewarding jobs, but many people (specifically many marginalised groups) are inevitably denied access to such opportunities.

In this chapter I have tried to establish the notion that what you see in the workplace is not always what you get, and that in recent decades it has becomes a sort of privileged ideological space for the reproduction of the consumer society. Let's think for a second about how the relatively tenuous hold of the workplace as an experience is maintained. One version of events is that all the insecurities and uncertainties to which I referred above are, as Southwood (2011) puts it, 'artificially maintained'. In this sense the whole manifestation of work as experience is a state of mind. This sense of perpetual precariousness is presented to us as non-negotiable; as an inevitable consequence of social change. We are, according to Southwood, paralysed into a mode of bemused inaction: told that the world of work is an endless phantasmagoria of possibility, choice and self-branding, when the mundane reality is more likely one of repetition, frustration and career progressions that are always just out of our reach:

> Such preoccupations divert attention away from wider abstract social or political concerns and on to a continual anxious self-surveillance. The constant precariousness and restless mobility, compounded by a dependence upon relentlessly updating market-driven technology and the scrolling CGI of digital media, suggest a sort of cultural stagnation, a population revving up without getting anywhere. The result

is a kind of frenetic inactivity; we are caught in a cycle of non-stop inertia. (Southwood, 2011: 11)

The point here is twofold. First, human beings are complicit in all of this. We are married to this world of uncertainty and insecurity, it's what we know: we struggle with the everyday realities of such a world and however much we might grumble about it, we mostly accept it passively and uncritically. Second, the emergence of the workplace as a stage for experiential self-exploration is a double-edged sword. The worker is expected to grin and bear the strains of the contemporary workplace while reassuring him and herself that however stressed and anxious they might feel things are not so bad after all because work's just better than it used to be, isn't it? There has been a significant rise in work-related mental health problems across Organisation for Economic Co-operation and Development nations (Tweedle, 2013). The expectation is that workers should simply cope. The problem is that the individualisation of work is actually undermining the degree to which they are able to do so.

Conclusion

Thirty years ago, during my student holidays, I worked at a meals-on-wheels factory close to my family home. Meals on wheels are the kind of meals that might be heated and delivered to older people unable to cook for themselves. My experience at the factory was eye opening and one aspect of my experience remains vivid in the memory. I worked on a production line. I would stand there, ice cream scoop in hand, placing a portion of peas into a passing aluminium tray alongside the other components of the meal that passed in front of me. What was interesting about this (though it didn't feel particularly so at the time) was how the factory employees were self-managed. There ensued a highly competitive atmosphere that ensured that the employees on one production line would constantly look to outdo their neighbours. They would do so by producing more meals than their competitors. There was no sense that this was something that was imposed by the management, it rather felt like a question of employee pride. As I discovered to my cost, woe betide any individual worker who was in any way responsible for interrupting the happy progress of the line. These employees appeared to be the authors of their own overworked demise. They effectively conspired to ensure their daily routine was unrelenting. The pseudo-excitement of the competition symbolised their complicity in the process in which they were engaged.

No doubt such working conditions still exist nationwide (and of course, in some parts of the world more than others). Certainly, there are more such places than the kind of future-thinking workspaces Borges et al. (2013) describe. However, the workplace is much changed, and there is no doubt that more attention is nowadays paid in the workplace to the individual experience. In the UK, for example, legislation on health and safety, unconscious bias and the like has certainly facilitated change for the good. But the point here, at the risk of stating the obvious, is that work is still work, and the individualisation of the workplace as far as the worker who has been privileged enough to experience it, inevitably does little more than camouflage that fact. The workplace has been reimagined, at least partially and as part of a broader unstable and unpredictable gig economy, as a place for personal exploration. But such exploration simply reinforces the power of capitalism to perpetuate the complicity of the employee.

Work is one of the primary arenas in which the experience society is played out. The impact of experience on the workplace, however, is also testament to an overriding impression that the benefits of such a society are inevitably partial: that, in other words, the availability of an experience and the consumer's ability to use that experience in the construction of self is tempered, as ever, by the social, cultural and economic circumstance in which the consumer finds him or herself. And even then it simply serves to extend the ways in which the worker can be exploited. In a world so tightly bound up with notions of aspiration and self-exploration we are nonetheless trained to believe that fulfilling work experiences are a right and that the inability to secure such a job should be something to be embarrassed about. I sit here as the most privileged of workers. Secure in the comfort zone of my sofa and free of the diversions of the office, I have had a productive working/ writing day. I feel like myself because it's through my writing that I feel that I am able to find myself. But who I am and what I am constructed of is not of my own making. It is the product of a world that frees me up and ties me down.

What all this adds up to is something of a mirage. The workplace cannot give us what we demand of it because capitalism is ahead of us in the queue. The world in which we live has created a curious state of affairs in which we have moved from looking to flee from work (as demonstrated by the workers' struggles of the 1960s and 1970s) to one in which work and our ability to maximise it has come to sit at the very core of our identity (Berardi, 2009). The shift that Berardi identifies here is one from something that used to be imposed via a hierarchy and which was a clearly defined task performed in exchange for wages to an increasingly digital and virtual workplace in which labour becomes a much more differentiated and mental process. In the case of the latter, what it means to be productive in such a workplace is much less clear and more troubling for the self.

Everyday life feels more exhausting and discomforting. It feels less and less like it is under our own personal control. Work provides one of the few viable escapes or outlets; one of the few places we feel we retain our worth as individuals (independent from the denial of self implied by familial responsibility, for example). The suggestion here is that the apparent reinvention of the workplace as an experience is the product of a broader structural change in which the self seeks solace, but the end product of which is actually a deepening of capitalist principles in which the worker is divided and ruled. It is in this sense that capitalism is a state of mind. The contemporary worker has thrown him/herself on the flames of experience. If there is one element of the new work that is most remarkable it is arguably that it has become so amorphous and deterritorialised, not least with the shift towards working from home (Berardi, 2009). It feels more fluid and less hierarchical because we are part of a big, less tangible whole in which network dependency comes to define us as working beings. In short,

> The intellectualization of labour, a major effect of the technologic and organisational transformation of the productive process ... opens completely new perspectives for self-realization. But it also opens up a field of completely new energies to the valorization of capital ... No desire, no vitality seems to exist anymore outside the economic enterprise, outside productive labour and business. Capital was able to renew its psychic, ideological and economic energy, specifically

thanks to the absorption of creativity, desire and individualistic, libertarian drives for self-realization. (Berardi, 2009: 96)

It is of course important to acknowledge the sheer diversity of the working experience. It would be ridiculous to claim that work is universally abhorrent and that any worker who perceives that his or her work experience has improved over time is delusional. But the point here is that the capacity for work to maximise the extent to which we are embedded in capitalist practice has been intensified by the ability of the capitalist workplace to put us at the centre of our own working experience.

André Gorz (1999) argues that social change was such that there was hope that our quest for identity might become less dependent upon work. This, I suggest, was a misguided assessment. Work is consumption. What has happened appears to be a shift in emphasis from the end of the twentieth century, in which consumption was catapulted to the top of the identity hierarchy, to the situation today, in which the workplace has reasserted its influence upon people's lives. It has done so by reinventing itself as a place in which workers can find and rejuvenate their consumer selves. By way of conclusion, I want to reinforce the notion that our intensified experience of work illustrates how much contemporary conceptions of work have come to be tied up in how we seek to bolster the self through processes of consumption. It is perhaps Christopher Lasch (1984: 27) who puts this most effectively:

> The social arrangements that support a system of mass production and mass consumption tend to discourage initiative and self-reliance and to promote dependence, passivity and a spectatorial state of mind both at work and at play. Consumerism is only the other side of the degradation of work – the elimination of playfulness and craftsmanship from the process of production.

Perhaps what we are talking about here is a state of affairs in which the boundaries between production and consumption have gradually become more blurred. Maybe the spectatorial state of mind to which Lasch refers constitutes a spectatorship of the self. In other words, what the experience of work allows us to do is to take a step outside ourselves in order to perceive who we are in the most positive of lights. Rightly or wrongly, I am abundantly conscious of how it is I work in order to construct a particular version of myself to be 'consumed' by colleagues. I quite often, for example, find myself wondering after a social event connected to work, whether I have given too much of myself by letting my guard down and in the process undermining the carefully curated self that I have produced. Work is both an experience and performance, and by seeking to balance the two we live the life that capitalism wants of us. The search for fulfilling work, the fulfilment that work as an experience can provide, is essentially a search for self. Not only that, it becomes so fundamental to who we are that when we have checked around to make sure none of our colleagues will notice as we skulk out of the office at 5 pm precisely, we close the door behind us in such a way that it's loss feels more permanent and more scarring than it ever has before. This is a loss that we experience to the full.

5

Technologies of Self

Technology provides the means by which we are able to create a world of our own making. As Gabriel and Lang put it, 'We now inhibit a digital world in which the technologies we use transform our ways of thinking, the ways we see ourselves and even our moral priorities' (Gabriel and Lang, 2016: 218). But the experience society is about more than just a transition from the consumption of objects to that of experience. It is actually more about a change in how consumption *feels*. Nowadays many of us appear to live in a virtual world as much as we do a real one; a world that constitutes an alternative space in which our identities are reconstituted and reimagined. In this world experience is everything, at least in the sense that it provides new possibilities for personalised selfhood through which we conspire to see the world through fresh experiential eyes. It is thus that the experience society has reinvented the relationship between self and consumption. Technology is the means by which the freedoms of the experience society are intensified and yet undermined at one and the same time. In the virtual space that technology has come to offer, the consumer is apparently liberated from the constraints of capitalism. But such liberation is nothing more than a daring falsehood, a falsehood that not only changes how we think but what we think, and it is on this falsehood that the myth of the self(ie) is built. The experience society is founded upon the conceit that it is through the escape technology provides that some semblance of authenticity can be procured; that by sacrificing ourselves to the virtual we can somehow find a sense of being that transcends the limitations of the physical world that came to be wholeheartedly defined *through* consumption. The experience society is in this sense a deeply ironic construction. It offers us the world and yet it painstakingly tempers that world, to the extent that the self we come to recognise through these means is barely any kind of a self at all.

The relationship between technology and consumption is a complicated one bound up with the subtleties of social change and its ideological implications. We would perhaps like to assume that technological change might bring with it the inevitability of progress in which the interests of human beings are best served. Current debates around artificial intelligence (AI) and its potential to undermine what it actually means to be human, on the other hand, might suggest otherwise. It is unclear whether AI is our mistress or our master. Moreover, as already pointed out, there has been a longstanding concern that consumption rather than production has become the organising principle of the society in which we live (Bauman, 1998). This is part of a historical process in which the working classes have become increasingly fragmented. Not only have many jobs gradually been taken away from human beings by so-called technological 'advancements', but class unity has been undermined in the process, partly as a result of being members of a society which says that the way to belong is through what we consume (Lodziak, 2002). The end product of this is a technology that perpetuates the very angst that it was perhaps designed to relieve.

In a world in which the relationship between work and consumption is subject to a constant process of reinvention, the role of digital technology is especially significant. It is not that experiences are inevitably digital, but rather that the digital has become so absolutely fundamental to how the self relates to experience. What's important here is the recognition that technology is not neutral; it is ideological. There might be some logic to assuming that the freeing up of the digital world would have some significant potential for political liberation and resistance. But such an assumption would, I want to argue, be misleading and potentially dangerous. As such, Kurylo (2018) considers the validity of Adorno's (1975) and Benjamin's (2008) contributions to debates around the technologisation of the twentieth century. Kurylo notes that unlike in Adorno's case, Benjamin suggests that, within it, technological developments hold the seeds of politicisation capable of liberating human beings from a life of drudgery. Benjamin argues that capitalist culture effectively creates new forms of communication based on this technology of mechanical reproduction, which in turn lead to a breakdown in traditional distinctions between the author and the consumer. Such distinctions erode the power of the aesthetic and create the potential for democratisation (see Swingewood, 1977). From this point of view the mass media has at least some potential as a force for positive social change. But alas, the intensification of the mass media's underpinning by technology means that this is perhaps less and less likely to be delivered.

Of course, over the last 80 or so years the media has developed in unimaginable ways. But far from this process empowering the consumer, despite and perhaps partly in light of the emergence of pro-sumption, the opposite has arguably been achieved. This can be partly understood as the by-product of a set of conditions in which technology increasingly emphasises the notion of *re*production as opposed to production (Jameson, 1991). Multinational network capitalism, as we know, is deeply complex and interlocking. It is effectively indecipherable. Castells (1996) identified in his 'network society' a virtual, multifaceted networked culture, that wasn't necessarily new in the sense that it was operationalising values that were long in the making. But what he saw emerge from all this was a culture of the ephemeral; one that was made up of what he calls 'a patchwork of experiences and interests' (1996: 214). This is a network that avoids rigidity for the economic good; a flexible network that is less about fantasy and more of a material force. By the 2010s the consumption of experiences had come to provide a more elegant means by which such a society could be reproduced. The long-term process that Castells describes is one in which the consumer becomes less and less passive, and more segmented and individualised. Such a transition was essential to the smooth running of a more effective, responsive economy, and inevitably a more divided society. The omnipresence of experience as the new playground in which consumption takes places is testament to the ability of that society to reinvent itself and to the vulnerability of consumers in being complicit in its affects.

But the indecipherability of technology is not imparted in an abstract space; it affects how we experience our everyday lives. As I have argued throughout this book, in some shape or form all consumption is experiential and technology plays a clear role in what and how we experience the world. Or at least, the way we conceive of technology as a means of constructing ourselves has itself been reimagined. Two authors who begin to come to terms with this is are McCarthy and Wright (2004), who talk about consumers' engagement with technology as a form of 'felt experience'. They argue that a transition has occurred from the consumption of computers, for example, as products that could do things for us, to products that operate in harmony with consumers' needs.

There is of course a significant design dimension to this. As a young PhD student I can recall the close relationship I had with my first 'real' computer, my Apple Macintosh. There was something about the look, the touch and the friendly interface that had a genuine effect on me. I engaged with that Mac in a way that I had never engaged with a computer before, nor since. And on reflection my experience of consuming the Mac was indicative of where the consumption of computer technology was going. Most importantly, the design of the Mac facilitated a kind of interactive engagement with the technology so that technology became more integrated into my everyday life. Computers came to feel more human, to the extent that my own mother sowed a green suede cover for my Mac so it could sleep peacefully at night. I didn't just use this technology, it became part of who I was: my PhD self. What I am describing here can in part be explained as the beginnings of what Zuboff (2019) refers to as 'the Apple inversion', which implies a reciprocity between commercial imperatives and the interests of the consumer:

> It held out the promise of a new digital market form that might transcend the collision: an early intimation of a third modernity capitalism summoned by the self-determining aspirations of individuals and indigenous to the digital milieu. The opportunity for 'my life, my way, at a price I can afford' was the human promise that quickly lodged at the very heart of the commercial digital project, from iPhones to one-click ordering to massive open online courses to on-demand services to hundreds of thousands of web-based enterprises, apps, and devices. (2019: 46)

This relationship between the dream and reality of technological change was not something that could be sustained. Apple became associated with high-end design that for many was simply out of the reach and, also notoriously, with Apple-specific add-ons at prices your average consumer had no chance of affording. As the company's finances went through the roof, so simultaneously did the broader digital realm, so that our ability to dream through technology was outpaced by the ability of technology to deliver.

It is no exaggeration to suggest that the digital world is not only transforming the world of consumption, but also how we as human beings relate to one another through the personalised platforms we construct around ourselves. For some commentators everyday life has effectively been 'virtualised', so that what is constructed online is as much a contributor as who we are offline, perhaps more so (Gabriel and Lang, 2016). Such a state of affairs is a key characteristic of the experience society insofar as technology is a constant feature of a rapidly changing information world. This is another sense in which the consumer is deterritorialised. His or identity is no longer located in time, space and place in the sense that we perhaps used to think. Time-space compression (Harvey, 1990) is such that the very notion of what constitutes a 'real' self has effectively been undermined. The digital world has reinforced this process to the extent that the core self is effectively lost between what exists of an actively digital person's real and the virtual self. In one sense this is all about a dematerialisation of consumption: a shift, as I suggested in Chapter 1, from the consumption of objects to that of experiences and an ever intensified engagement with a world beyond the materially mundane. But it isn't as straightforward as this may seem. Gabriel and Lang (2016) argue that time spent in front of a computer or on a tablet is time actually devoted to digital labour, characterised by the scene of a diverse and apparently and yet obscurely connected band of workers tapping away on their Apple Macs. More broadly this can be said to represent an intensification of work, so even when we feel we have escaped from the clutches of work, in practice we really are working, in the case of downloading music for example. Services such as Napster and more recently Spotify may have opened up the world of music to the consumer, but arguably there is a price to pay (Forde, 2019). Given the sheer excess of options with which the digital world provides the consumer, and the work this necessitates, the nature of the relationship between how we consume and who we are is arguably put under further intense strain.

Prosumption and Social Media

Today, prosumption, the process by which the barriers between production and consumption are being digitally redefined, is key insofar as material realties no longer limit the potential ways in which production and consumption might be fused (Zajc, 2015). Prosumption sits at the heart of any kind of a notion that the digital self can be in control of his or her own fate. The speed of the digital network provides the technological means by which a world of user-generated content can be produced and consumed by consumers virtually simultaneously. This blurring of the boundaries between work and consumption is perhaps most evident in how consumers interact with social media. Forty per cent of the world's population currently uses it, updating profiles, liking and disliking, precariously sharing the mundane detail, of everyday life (Seymour, 2019). It is true, as Kurylo (2018) points out, that digital media has served to blur the boundaries between production and consumption, and that this process could be said to have significant advantages: making technology more accessible and, indeed, potentially more agentic insofar as traditional patterns of production and reception are broken down (e.g. through the consumption of music). But such a conclusion would be partial one.

Prosumption builds upon a set of processes that had already trans-formed the world of media such that by the 1980s the individualisation of such media was becoming more and more of a reality, and a commer-cialised one at that (Castells, 1996). However, to overgeneralise from such a statement would be ill-advised. Accessibility does not equate to emancipation, not least given the observation that, 'The audience itself, its consumption habits and search history, has long been the principal commodity on sale while receiving no pay in return' (Kurylo, 2018: 8–9). The point here is that technology sells agency, or at least the appear-ance of agency. The meanings that can be accumulated by consumers through technology and in particular through digitalised consumption are apparently infinite. But crucially, as Kurylo points out, such forms of liberation come at a significant cost, in the form of what she calls 'a more omnipotent control' (2018: 9). However much prosumption might problematise the balance of the relationship between the consumer and the producer, what it does *not* do is question the authority of the market. This is a crucial point and one I want to explore throughout this chapter, namely that even if we accept that technology might open up the range of experiences in which the consumer can participate, and however much it might provide opportunities for self-endowment, ultimately such experiences are imaginary insofar as what they do, and all they can do, is propel the individual into a world of imaginary (capitalist) possibilities (see Illouz, 2009).

Digital consumption provides a platform upon which consumers can access simulated sensations of belonging (Kurylo, 2018). Another way of putting this, as Kurylo suggests when considering the work of Buck-Morris (1992), is as a 'sensory addiction to a compensatory reality' (Kurylo, 2018: 23) that operates primarily as a means of social control. However much politicians might berate the world of fake news, there is surely an argument for suggesting that political lines are being redrawn, often outside those lines established by traditional political parties. However, the extent to which such changes add up to any genuine kind of liberation on the part of the consumer to control his or her own news is highly questionable. Rather, technological innovation has massively increased the potential for the manipulation of consumers. This is not to say that consumers have absolutely no choice in such matters, nor that they are unable to endow technological experiences with their own meanings, but rather that their ability to do so masks a process in which the ideological power of consumer capitalism is intensified. And this intensification comes about because social media is fundamentally a form of technology that operates in the name of the production of distraction. Social media are designed to provide unending opportunities for new forms of fascination, self-styling and 'thinking-as-leisure-time' (Seymour, 2019).

The Digital Self

In an experience society the experience of selfhood is intensified. The high cultural profile, indeed the omnipresence of the selfie, is testament to this. Why experience an event, when you can experience that event through your smartphone? It is in this context that Storr (2018) argues that if we are to be attuned to the economic and therefore the cultural demands of the society in which we live from birth, its values are inevitably reproduced *through* us and thus through how we choose to engage with technology. Indeed, 'Neoliberalism beams at us from many corners of our culture and we absorb it back into ourselves like radiation' (Storr, 2018: 263). In such a culture, social media, and selfies in particular, provide a means of self-validation: they demonstrate how the seeking of such validation from strangers serves to actively prop up the self. The self has effectively become a fluid abstraction. It is now networked, and thus subject to a more complex process of negotiation and affirmation than would have been the case in a pre-digital world. Technology, and in particular social media platforms, provide a stage upon which the self can be presented (Papacharissi, 2011). The material technology that makes this possible, the mobile phone, is constantly at our side as we enter a perennial and ever more immediate cycle of comparing our selves with others (Storr, 2018). But for Storr, technology, and social media in particular, is about much more than just appearance. It is gamifying the self so that identity becomes little more than a pawn. Founded on the delusion that under the conditions of the market, all are equal, the consumer finds him or herself in a perpetual chase for likes, feedback and friends. This is a world of expressive connectedness: a world in which experiences are constructed performatively and according to which audience the individual is trying to please (Papacharissi, 2011).

It is in the above sense that the technological experience has been embroidered and intensified, or to put this another way experience is now triangulated: our experience of the world is not only the product of what we consume, but of how we are seen to consume, not simply by those around us but as bit-part players in the networked society in which we are implicated. As Papacharissi notes, this results in a kind of deterritorialised placelessness that far from resulting in an emptying out of experience actually serves to multiply its significance. The experience is intensified because it has become the product of overlapping relationships which feel more real than the real world itself. The process implicates the individual through the intangibility of the virtual collective: a virtual collective that is actually less about the individual and more about how that individual is stylised and self-branded.

MeTube

Of all the forms of social media available, YouTube appears to be gaining more and more traction as a go-to platform for young people. As such, Farokhmanesh (2018) quotes a recent study conducted by the Pew Research Center which found that 85 per cent of teenagers (ages 13–17) use the platform. Closely behind were Instagram (72 per cent) and Snapchat (69 per cent). Noting that 95 per cent of teenagers compared to 73 per cent in 2015 now have smartphones, the suggestion is that YouTube has the potential to make young people feel good about themselves. Most importantly, they apparently feel they can relate to YouTubers or influencers, almost as if they were just regular people that they just happened to come across in their everyday lives (Stone, 2015).

Meanwhile, it's interesting to note that this isn't a purely youthful phenomena, and that Facebook is becoming the go-to social networking site for older people, with around 6.5 million Facebook users aged over 55 in a given year (Sweney, 2018). All this reflects a state of affairs in which the digital public culture in which consumers engage, has become increasingly user-generated and participatory, diversifying the nature of consumption that this implies in the process. The underlying imperative that underpins YouTube in particular is apparently all about community, authenticity and vernacular culture (Burgess and Green, 2013). But this all comes at a cost: such platforms have become increasingly adept at aggregating and exploiting data, and thus curating experience to best serve the business logics that underpin them, as part of what some commentators have dubbed the platformisation of society (Van Dijck et al., 2018). The point here is that digital forms of identity construction perpetuate a situation in which experience is both mediated and lived. As such, 'digital self-construction or self-presentation makes it possible to express latent identities or disclose aspects of the self that are difficult to represent physically and more fully' (Chen, 2016: 235).

The power inherent in social media to construct and reproduce social norms is clearly profound. Such platforms do not simply reflect the realities of our time; they actively produce them through the maintenance of social structures (Van Dijck et al., 2018). Such a process can be manifested in a whole host of unpredictable ways, but the point is that these are almost inevitably filtered through the commodity. For example, Toffoletti and Thorpe (2017) discuss the way in which female athletes use Instagram as a means of branding themselves in the global sporting marketplace. By doing so they are able to create a connection with their fanbase, a sense of intimacy and authenticity through what could perhaps best be described as 'aesthetic labour' (Elias, 2008). The legitimacy of using the female body in this way is reproduced so that this becomes more than just an economic entity, but also a cultural one. As Toffoletti and Thorpe put it, 'Instagram posts that are accorded the most value in the fan–athlete interaction – that is, receive the most visibility in terms of likes and comments – are modes of expression that align most closely to wider social attitudes about the qualities young women today are expected to possess' (2017: 313).

There is a delicate balance here in which the poise between private and public benefit is effectively policed by the internet. Of course, a primary concern in this regard is that although our experience of such platforms as consumers is reasonably enabling on the surface, you don't have to dig too deep to realise that this equates to a deal with the devil, who busily goes about his business collecting infinite amounts of data about our online patterns of behaviour. Zuboff (2019) thus describes the 'mercenaries of the self' who go about packaging the self in the interests of what she calls 'surveillance revenues'. And the irony here is that the more the consumer seeks a personalised experience the more the self is lost to the machines seeking to prescribe what that self needs. In this regard, the process of personalisation is particularly worrisome. People are attracted to platforms precisely because they personalise their experience: they allow access to what a consumer is looking for via the quickest possible route. But such freedoms not only mean that behind the scenes all kinds of personal data are collected in the interests of predictive choice, but they may also limit our experience by deciding what such experience should be (Van Dijck et al., 2018; Pariser, 2011).

In light of the kind of invasion and definition of personal space we are talking about here, YouTube is not the neutral web service it might reasonably have claimed to have been in the past. Indeed, it would nowadays be far-fetched to suggest that YouTube delivered the kind of democratised culture that some of its earlier exponents imagined for it. As Burgess and Green (2013) also point out, although earlier discourses around YouTube were bound up around utopian notions of folk culture, and the onus on user participation that this implied, such inclinations were never able to wriggle free of the broader logics of vast media empires deeply sensitive to the economic potential of the audiences they were creating. As a cultural space that has sought to establish its own sets of participatory norms and practices, YouTube is fraught with contradiction. The sense of intimacy and community that it has created is ultimately one that serves the interests of a higher power in which the needs of consumers are nothing more than a means to an end.

But what does all this mean for the consumer? What's interesting here, as Storr (2018) points out, is that this obliges consumers, and particularly young people, to buy into a culture in which perfection is deemed to be a necessary norm. And however real all this is we accept it as *being* real. We don't question this state of affairs, we live it to the full. We don't so much live our selves, as get fixated by them. This is an increasingly narcissistic world, an age of perfectionism in which our focus on the self and a blind belief in progress allows us to hide away from the terrifying realities of social change. And the point is that the space created through this process is not a neutral space but one that is deluged by the finger-prints of marketers so that how we interact, how we communicate and how we socialise are profit-making acts in their own right.

A New Capitalism?

If you took the world of technologised digital consumption at face value you might conclude that the possibilities for individualised self-enhancement are 'virtually' endless. It could indeed be argued that the age of digital capitalism is indicative of a new immaterial existence which, paradoxically, suggests a triumphant capitalism, but one that is simultaneously dissolved (Betancourt, 2015). Such a proclamation might sound extreme but it hints at the paradoxical set of circumstances that we are trying to understand. For Betancourt, a new magical realm of the digital has been opened that appears to free the individual from physical constraints, while implying a perpetual expansion of wealth. It is in this sense that the power of the digital realm lies less in its ability to expand consumer choice and more in the expansion of the illusion of consumer choice (see also Zajc, 2015). The individual is no longer what they consume, but rather what narrative they present to the world about how and what it is they consume (Theodoridis et al., 2019). By opening up an arena that is characterised by a whole range of new forms of economic production, the very meaning that underpins the society in which we live comes to be defined by a massive intensification of the commodification of social life; a social life no longer constrained by space and place. This is a society that transcends the physical limitations of reality (Betancourt, 2015). The emphasis here on fantasy is crucial. The digital sphere provides capitalism with the illusion of 'accumulation without capitalism' (Betancourt, 2015: 87) and it's this which gives it its ideological power:

> Thus, the aura of the digital is Janus-like, suggesting a magical pro-duction without consumption, reifying this fundamental ideology as digital capitalism, at the same time as it implies an elision of capital-ism itself. However, all these suggestions proceed from an illusion based in a refusal to acknowledge the real expenditure required in

the creation, production, maintenance and access to the digital technologies and the materials made available through these technologies which make these ideological fantasies possible. (Beatancourt, 2015: 59)

Perhaps digital capitalism is better understood as an attempt to *deny* physicality rather than as an *escape* from it. It's in this part of his analysis that Betancourt puts his finger on the key to this discussion. Yes, of course, we need to understand the rise of digital capitalism in a historical context. But the virtual nature of digital consumption and the implications it has for meaning and identity making does not constitute a radical break with the past or a killing off of the realm of the physical but rather 'its stripping from consciousness' (2015: 218). None of this is a surprise as far as the evolution of capitalism is concerned, given it always has and always will be about colonising new spaces and arenas, of the physical variety or otherwise. But what is important here is not so much the emergence of the digital as a new sphere of consumption and thus of ideological intent, but the fact it is able to emerge in such a way that its ideological significance is barely noticed.

It is worth reflecting on the above, albeit briefly, from the perspective of a specific technological product. The question of escape is put further under the microscope in the work of Michael Bull (2007), who reflects upon the Apple iPod as the first 'cultural icon' of the twenty-first century. The iPod as a form of technology is already effectively redundant, which in being so highlights the transitory nature of technology and its ability to privatise cultural experience. Of course, the iPod is an object, but it's an object that arguably transforms how the consumer interacts with the world insofar as it makes the consumer the author, rather than the receiver, of his or her own sound experience or 'auditory worship' (2007: 2–3). The iPod is experiential insofar as it allows the individual to construct their own individualised sonic life experience, an 'auditory bubble' and most of all a sense of control. Thus, Bull talks about iPod users as living in a world of mediated we-ness: in other words, in building upon the work of Adorno (1991a), Bull (2007) draws attention to how technologically mediated experience has become a substitute for direct experience. Bull discusses Adorno's assertion that music provides a means for the subject to transcend the oppressive nature of the social world. In this way music provides an outlet by which consumers can experience what they desire without achieving it in any substantive way so that it produces 'an illusion of immediacy in a totally mediated world, of proximity between strangers, the warmth of those who come to feel a chill of unmitigated struggle of all against all' (Horkheimer and Adorno, 1972: 46). The sense of belonging implied here is illusory (as indeed are the communities that social media apparently offer). It would perhaps be an exaggeration to suggest that we should thus conclude that the consumer of the iPod and other such technological avenues of individualised escapism are entirely futile. But the notion that music can in itself be an escape, a means of authentic selfhood, is at least one worthy of challenging. And in this sense perhaps technology represents the means by which consumer capitalism has been further able to blur the boundaries between subjectivity and objectivity.

A recognition that the ability of capitalism to reinvent itself is becoming more sophisticated is crucial if we are to begin to understand the changing nature of the self. Denegri-Knott and Molesworth (2012) thus call upon the work of Rob Shields (2003) in arguing that digital virtual consumption lacks material substance. This effectively frees up the consumer in such a way that within that space anything and everything becomes possible, even that which is not possible in the reality of the everyday. A consumer can build a virtual home that may not provide them with real-life shelter, but what it can do is provide the parameters within which they are untouched by the constraints of real life (e.g. planning laws, the availability of such housing on the market). The result is a heady space in which selfhood, deliberately or otherwise, enters new realms of impossibility: a self-performative space in which, as Shields (2003) notes, the potential for self-transformation is 'supercharged'. In short, digital virtual consumption provides a means for experimentation and transformation that unburdens the individual from the everyday, possibly allowing them to partake in transgressive activities that wouldn't normally be available to them. But it does so in a fashion that is intimately tied to, or as Denegri-Knott and Molesworth (2012) put it, 'wired into', commodities and consumer experiences. Such experiences feel liberating and all-encompassing, and in this a sense of freedom control is able to reside more easily. Lehdonvirta (2012) thus argues that digital virtual goods serve the same purpose as their material counterparts as part of an acceleration of capitalism, but do so in a way that is more honest insofar as they rely less heavily on the symbolic power of branded goods. They do not pretend to meet some basic human need: they are often about providing the consumer with a self-conscious mode of escape. Another way of putting this might be that digital virtual consumption is characterised by a certain playfulness that perhaps offers the consumer a subtlety of unbounded experience that they cannot access elsewhere (Molesworth and Denegri-Knott, 2012).

There is indeed a debate as to whether or not digital virtual consumption inevitably reinforces and extends the alienated ways in which consumers experience the world through commodities. But my argument is that it does so much more than this: precisely because digital forms of consumption are playful, precisely because they exaggerate the pleasure to be had by engaging in such arenas, precisely because they free consumers up to feel that they can play freely. These are the reasons that, ideologically speaking, they are such powerful places. It is through digital virtual consumption that the consumer is perhaps most able to experience freedom (Molesworth and Denegri-Knott, 2012). This in turn allows the consumer to 'craft' consumption in such a way that they can build relationships with others through consumption. In doing so they may be able to fashion a degree of control over this aspect of their lives that they may not be able to do elsewhere. This is precisely where the attraction of the experience society resides. It is through experience that consumer citizenship utilises a sense of belonging that can in turn justify a mental absenteeism from the demands of everyday life.

What technology tells us about the experience society is that it is all-encompassing. To put it another way, it engulfs the individual. This isn't a straightforward case of the consumer being duped into behaving in a machine-like fashion. This is more than a straightforward example of twenty-first century narcissism. The picture I am trying to draw here is one in which the consumer is more and more susceptible to the allure of the consumer society. By jumping into the ocean of individualised consumption that the experience society implies he or she unwittingly puts him or herself directly in the sights of capitalist imperialism.

Live Streaming as Emotional Experience

My discussion of social media above demonstrates how the ability of technology to set parameters around how we consume is becoming increasingly sophisticated. What technology does, as McCarthy and Wright (2004) suggest, is intensify what it is we already do, in this case the intensification of communication, while commodifying elements of experience that we would not have previously considered to be commodifiable. Perhaps the best recent example of this process and how it is so quintessentially experiential is the live streaming of video games (Taylor, 2018). Reaching over 100 million viewers per month, live streaming is a form of interactive entertainment that incorporates big esports events with digital game players being live streamed globally. Real-time chat means this amounts to what is a highly interactive experience. It involves a sharing of experiential flow and in particular the sharing of a whole range of emotions between player and audience. Taylor describes this as the transformation of private play into public entertainment: the amplification of mundane experience so that the audience buy into a shared sense of presence and belonging. Live streaming offers a collective social experience that can have significant personal implications:

> Watching your favourite esports player's live stream is about like what you might imagine it's like to watch your favourite baseball player practice for hours a day. Though mundane, it can also be riveting. Audiences get to view pro players practice their game, refine strategies, and reflect on their own play along with that of the competitors they encounter during a session. For those watching the stream, this can be a powerful learning tool, tapping into competitive aspirations or the hope to improve one's play. (Taylor, 2018: 82)

Taylor goes on to describe what he calls a 'circuit of affective labour' that flows through live streaming: fans, moderators and broadcasters and the like creating a symbiotic 'buzz' of gelled experience. But this does not come without a price. The hazing of production and consumption involved here turns private pleasures into forms of labour and as such intensifies the malleability of the consumer (see also Kreiss et al., 2011). Taylor goes on to discuss the possibility that the principle of play has been corrupted by such developments. And yet he nonetheless contends that those involved in gaming are engaged in the construction of 'authentic meaning', and as such make social connections which in turn imply forms of social and individual transformation. I consider this to be an optimistic reading of the current state of play (as it were). Yes, meaning-making can be facilitated in an experience society, but the point is that the more meaning can be made, the more the experience of that meaning can be commodified for the greater economic good.

In short, technology has become more and more about what consumers feel as opposed to what they do, so that 'it is not the abstract idea of communicating, perhaps not even the social practice, but the felt and sensual quality of the particular communication that give it an expressive quality' (Taylor, 2018: 13). You might ask, why label this the 'experience society' rather than, say, the 'feeling society'? What technology tells us about the nature of consumption and how it ties us to social structures is that the way we feel about what we consume has been reimagined in an experiential realm. This has significant consequences not only for who we are, but also in terms of how who we are can be appropriated in the best interests of consumer capitalism. As McCarthy and Wright put it, 'this is where we locate the playfulness of experience. It is in the simultaneously aesthetic consummation of an other as a centre of value separate from ourselves that we play with our own selves, making dialogical moments complex, deep and open' (2004: 188). For Zuboff (2019), experience is less about what is given to the consumer and more about what they make of what is given to them. It is an inward space in which we have the facility to construct meaning. But the suggestion is not that this inner space is sacrosanct. 'Surveillance capitalism' is not content with simply maximising sales. It wants to know anything and everything it can know. Zuboff (2019) goes as far as to argue that the market that the digital world creates manages to disguise itself as a mirror of the consumer's self, apparently metamorphosing according to our needs, while always delivering on its own, 'What happens when they come for my "truth" uninvited and determined to march through my self, taking the bits and pieces that can nourish their machines to reach their objectives. Cornered in my, self, there is no escape' (2019: 291)

The experience society allows us to go some way to finding out who it is we are. But it insists we do so through the lens of consumer capitalism. Unfortunately consumer capitalism has no scruples in this regard. Prosumption isn't about liberating the consumer. It's about creating a society in which we are always working so that even our escapism is nothing more than another form of labour; digital labour (Gabriel and Lang, 2016). I buy from Amazon. I work for Amazon. I am Amazon.

And ultimately the illusion of experience does nothing more than feed the capitalist machine so that individualisation can never be anything more than an Amazonian delivery of an inglorious worldwide algorithm of the selfless self, because ultimately the selfless self is an economically productive self. Technology does not liberate us, it ties us to the very system from which we seek escape (Seymour, 2019).

Conclusion

We cannot understand any of this without locating it in the broader context of neoliberalism and its impact upon the reinvention of citizenship. Jayne Raisborough (2011) discusses how the liberal approach to economics and its emphasis on the benefits of the free market – its onus on the self-interest of individuals and the existence of an entrepreneurial self – created a particular version of citizenship. That this was a kind of citizenship that was all about the ability of the individual to be fit, flexible and enterprising no matter what the market sent in their direction. The onus is therefore on the self to be agile in the shadow of the demanding conditions that a market-based economy creates. It's in this context that self-transformation and self-realisation came to be appropriated as the ideological underpinning of neoliberalism (Raisborough, 2011). Such an ideology, in turn, argues Raisborough, created a set of circumstances in which the citizens of such a society came to believe that as long as you have consumer choice, anything is possible. Neoliberalism effectively 'demands and forges new relationships between the self, capitalism and the state' (Raisborough, 2011: 14). What our discussion of technology in this chapter has drawn attention to is the way in which the internet and communication technologies have resulted in a reimagination of identities in more dynamic forms (Rattle, 2014). Indeed, Rattle wonders about the extent to which such changes have not only changed the way in which material identities are constructed, but have potentially created a set of circumstances in which such identities are less readily identified with notions of individualism, and perhaps even less easily defined through consumption than they were in the past.

The short life cycle of technology-related products and the regular upgrading and technological 'lock-in' that they demand, potentially accelerates and intensifies the set of conditions through which commodification can determine consumers' identities (Rattle, 2014). The internet and communication technologies increase our dependence on a world that emphasises the material expression of identity, a process that is further reinforced by complex computer algorithms that know more about how to maximise how we might spend than we would surely appreciate. The sum total of all this is a process of 'supracommodification' which is solely concerned with the instantaneous maximisation of profit (Rattle, 2014). In one sense this is a world of competition, of friends and likes, but in another sense it is one of collaboration and cooperation. What Rattle describes here is a radical transformation in the nature of the relationship between consumption and identity; a relationship that raises many questions about the role of what and how we might consume in the future. Indeed, 'Internet and communication technologies have given birth to an emerging consumer culture capable of functioning not as mere aggregation of individual consumers each imagining, defining, constructing and re-constructing identity, but as a self-aware, globally synchronized consumer culture' (Rattle, 2014: 136).

The truth is, as Rattle himself notes, the production and consumption of consumer identity formation remains materially determined in many key respects. But what's interesting about this analysis is the proposition that what's actually changing here is the 'how', as opposed to the 'what', of consumer-based identity formation, the result of which is that 'the material is becoming less the objective and more the means in identity formation' (Rattle, 2014: 138). This could be interpreted as a liberating process of group-based experience making; a dilution of individualism and a technological opening up of choice. One version of events is that despite all the doubts I have expressed above about how digital experience might undermine our sense of self in a networked society, social media platforms and the like are ultimately liberating in their effect. We could perhaps regard the digital as a liminal space in which we can build a fantasy version of ourselves (Turkle, 2011). Or indeed, fantasy versions. The experiences we can access though our digital lives allow us to construct multiple selves that would not otherwise be available to us, and who is to say this is a bad thing?

The problem with the above analysis is that it fails to comprehend the digital self as sufficiently social. It effectively buys into the very neoliberal ideology to which I draw attention. The technologies that we are tied to in an experience society primarily implicate the consumer in a process of maximising the number of experiences in which they engage, first and foremost as a means of accumulating a sense of affirmation and belonging. Digital forms of consumption are less about binding us together and more about preoccupying us in a never-ending zero-sum game of choice (Turkle, 2011). Social media, not least as propagated by the smartphone, keeps us busy so that our brains are constantly rewired and fully experienced, as each and every moment passes us by at one and the same time. In one sense it is impossible to freely construct a so-called authentic self. The 'purity' of the self, if such a thing can ever be achieved, is mitigated by the platform on which it is presented or exchanged. The online environment is studiously demanding and riddled with expectations to which all participants are obliged to respond. Moreover, the digital self is not constructed in a vacuum but in relationship to distanced others (Rybas, 2012). In other words, the culture of experience with which the consumer engages online is not free at all. It is inevitably managed, prescribed and predetermined. In discussing the work of the Frankfurt School, Stuart Jeffries (2016) mentions the philosopher Friedrich Kittler who points out that we are obliged to adapt to technology and not it to us. From this point of view, ruminates Jeffries, technological innovation simply persuades us to jump from one meaningless endeavour to another 'like victims of a Sisyphean curse' (2016: 184). The internet would, on this basis, surely constitute another means, an apparatus, by which the unreal world constructed by commodity capitalism is fatalistically taken to be *real*.

In many ways, the world of technology surely enhances what it means to be a human being. As such this debate is more complicated than the above argument might initially suggest. Technology isn't all bad. The problem is not *that* we engage with it, but *how* we engage with it; it is that the intense way in which digital forms of consumption pray on our time is both deeply ingrained in our culture and in our psyche. Its everyday attraction to us is therefore deeply compelling and leads to authors such as Newport (2019) to call for moves towards a digital minimalism in which we focus our online time on a much smaller number of optimised tasks which strongly support the things we value, 'By working backward from their deep values to their technology choices, digital minimalists transform these innovations from a source of distraction into tools to support a life well lived. By doing so, they break the spell that has made so many people feel like they're losing control to their screens' (Newport, 2019: 29).

Such sentiments hint at the more innocent, less technologically determined times of a bygone age. They reflect a longstanding debate around consumption that basically says, less is more. What we are talking about here is not in fact a question about quantity at all. Newport argues that the world of techno-maximalism in which we live is essentially mindless. We sign up to its personal invasions as though that it is the most natural thing in the world and in the process we 'outsource our liberty' and 'degrade our individuality' (Newport, 2019: 58). But there is something more profound going on here. The experience society doesn't simply persuade us to consume in particular ways, it convinces us that by doing so we are wringing as much as we can out of the world in which we live. What a consideration of technology as experience tells us is that we live in a society that is not only very accomplished at providing us with experiences that feel real, but is also quite capable of creating a kind of virtual reality that we are convinced is preferable to our own. The experience society sells us a world in which experience trumps everything. It encourages us to believe we are free to lose and find ourselves simultaneously through what it is we experience. This is not an achievable goal. It only succeeds insofar as it ties our sense of self to the very system from which we feel virtual space can liberate us. As far as consumption is concerned the key role of technology has perhaps been to reassert its pivotal place at the heart of how human beings experience social change in the everyday. This may or may not be a good thing, but it can certainly be said to intensify the potential influence of consumption as what is primarily ideological terrain.

In exploring the notion of the digital self, Belk (2013: 479) argues that the digital transforms the ways 'we represent ourselves, get to know other people, and interact'. For Belk, in a digital world where the idea of a core self is undermined by multiple online personas, the *illusion* of a core self remains very strong. Another way to put this might be to argue that we live in an ever more privatised world in which shared notions of self have an increasingly powerful impact on how we see ourselves. It is also important to remember that the world we access through the digital, via say Second Life, is not the same as what Belk (2014) describes as the 'embodied' experience. We feel empowered by the digital world and the products that it incorporates because of who and what it can help us become rather than by the products themselves. As Belk points out, the impact of the digital on the self is significant precisely because it is more about the doing than the having. And if there is one key characteristic of the experience society this is it. By consuming the digital we aspire to create a self greater than the sum of our physical parts. But the truth is: the body is everything. What we ultimately achieve is the construction of an alternative world in which the lack of a material being heightens the possibility of ideological control.

As Marcuse (1986: 437) put it in his book *Reason and Revolution*, 'Technological progress multiplied the needs and satisfactions, while its utilisation made the needs as well as their satisfactions repressive: they themselves sustain submission and domination.' From a Marxist point of view the rising standards of living that technological advancement have evidently produced have effectively made the working classes too comfortable to revolt (Jeffries, 2016; Lodziak, 1995). At one level we can thus identify the automation of work and the dominance of the machine which have served to create a situation in which the same volume of goods can be produced by less workers. It's in this context that Lodziak quotes Frank Mort (1989), who argues that consumption is important because it makes people *feel* powerful. The experience society takes this sense of individualised power to a whole new level. What Seymour (2019) calls *The Twittering Machine* is ultimately defined by what has become a smartphone-driven world of amusement and entertainment that has come to colonise our lives. It does so in the name of experience, and it is to this that we are addicted.

6

Space, Place and the
Architecture of Experience

Space and place are not neutral entities. They are the constantly evolving product of a capitalism that perpetually seeks to maximise its potential. Spaces for consumption are in no way innocent; they are constructed – built not to fulfil our needs, but rather to fulfil needs that we never knew we had. The way we consume is not a natural state of affairs, but a state of affairs that over several decades has come to *feel* real. And the prominence of our own experiences in how we engage with physical space is what allows consumer capitalism and the obligations it puts on us to feel more real than ever. The impact of the experience society on space and place is about giving and taking away, and arguably the overwhelmed loser in this process is the so-called sovereign consumer.

We live in a world of place branding and of city making in which the trick is to convert heterogeneous environments into personalised experiences and manipulate symbols in the wilful construction of identities (Subramanian, 2017; Govers and Go, 2009; Landry, 2006). The relationship between market and place is tattooed into our very urban existence, and it is the kind of tattoo that cannot be easily removed. Authors like Zukin have long written about how the globalisation of markets has diminished space, arguing that 'The spatial consequences of combined social and economic power suggest that landscape is the major cultural product of our time' (1991: 22). This is a process that has promoted consumership over citizenship, creating spaces that inevitably advantage some actors and social groups at the expense of others, while all the time ensuring that consumption is a key means of socialisation. Such a process hides the role of centralised economic power through the veneer of spaces for consumption and the false promises that they provide. The pleasures of experience are an increasingly intense characteristic of our relationship to places and spaces, and the more that they are so, the less tangible becomes our relationship to the power bases that created them. Herein lies the power of the experience society.

This world that we have constructed for ourselves has significant consequences insofar as it sows the seeds for what is a particular intensification of 'consumership'. This notion is explored, for example in the work of Hayward (2004), who argues that individual subjective emotions are generated by social conditions and cultural codes, not least at the moment through consumption codes. Markets give such a fundamental role to how we perceive cities that they become a physical and emotional manifestation of consumerism as an ideology. Meanwhile, consumerism (e.g. through advertising) actively cultivates particular tendencies that may ultimately be expressed, from Hayward's criminological perspective, in forms of 'expressive criminal behaviour' (2004: 11). In this process 'the subject' has been left asunder, not least as a result of the destruction of the social contract that previously characterised modernity. We live in a society defined by the rewards on offer and underpinned by a consumerism that includes and excludes, but which above all is spatially varied in its effect as consumerism fills the void of a society bereft of the certainties that modernity used to provide. Even if you are able to access the freedoms that the city of consumption provides, the extent to which capitalist appropriation can deliver the benefits it promises are highly questionable, given the homogenised city that it tends to create (Klingmann, 2007).

Architecture and Experience

Architecture is a primary vehicle by which the experience society is delivered. It could indeed be argued that buildings and how we relate to them not only constitute part of the way the environment is marketed, but equate to the essence of it (Klingmann, 2007). The notion of architecture as a 'vehicle' draws attention to the fact that architecture is far more than we might see of it on the surface. Indeed, the word architecture is itself insufficient given that what architecture delivers is so tied up with other processes such as politics, regeneration, neoliberalism, place branding, class division, cultural capital and the like that it is virtually impossible to isolate, certainly at any kind of a causal level. Architecture is subject to fashion, but more importantly it is subject to the power dimensions of the society in which it operates (Jones, 2011). Architecture is the vehicle of the experience society insofar as it constitutes the manifestation of that society's physical form. More importantly, at its most cutting edge architecture is a visible reminder of where that society is and where it is going. In what follows, I am concerned with the way in which architecture reproduces dominant modes of thought, and specifically how it does so through the prism of the experience society.

What is it that defines the contemporary city and where does experience fit into that evolving definition? One way of understanding the city is as a liberating space, one that allows the individual to thrive in the anonymity of the unexpected urban encounter. This is a city of desire and of fantasy in which we are enticed out of the security of our everyday routines to embrace the strange and the surprising (see Sandercock, 1998). In contemplating it in this way the city becomes a place of excitement and of opportunity: a city of dreams. And as Sandercock argues, the significance of all this lies in the fact that by implication the city becomes less about needs and more about a personal engagement with place through dreams and feelings. Such sentiments seem to imply that what I describe as the experience society is founded upon the essence of humanity: the desire to explore what it is that makes us human through the unexpected. But the problem here is that the experience society isn't about the liberation of the human spirit at all. It is rather about the exploitation of that spirit for economic benefit. Herein lies the bind in which architecture finds itself. The 'calling' of architecture lies, as Chaplin and Holding (1998) point out, in the aspiration to achieve a harmonious, well-designed existence, and yet architecture's own existence has come to be defined by the opposite: social progress is inevitably stymied when consumption is its underlying impetus, and yet without consumption architecture has nowhere to go. In fact, you could also argue that the city's obsession with experience effectively undermines any notion we might have had of the city as a communal whole. It becomes little more than an amalgam of points of sale in which human connection and community are sacrificed (Sorokin, 1992).

In reflecting on its own self-importance, architecture, or at least architects, always dwell on the design-driven as opposed to the commercially driven element of their enterprise. You only have to navigate around a typical architectural degree show to see where these seeds are sown. The 'designs' that graduating students present are rarely of extensions, garages or modest social housing provision, but are more likely to be fantastical visions of futuristic spinach-fuelled constructions that have little or no chance of ever becoming a reality, at least not in the next 200 years. Meanwhile, even the most significant of architects whose work is perhaps most indicative of the time, such as Jon Jerde for example, are devalued or considered less worthy because of their (often playful) commitment to the commercial world upon which, in reality, architecture so depends. The product of all this is, as Chaplin and Holding (1998) suggest, a distorted architecture, one that frames the very world that it so apparently detests. For them architecture's relationship with experience is about the management of consumption space, or what you might call a mechanical choreography that says less about human beings actual living in space and more about 'experiencing' it, the latter being effectively a pale imitation of the former:

> Many of the projects built for consumers, for the sake of retail or entertainment, are deemed by the influential, elite end of the profession to be populist and therefore outside the normal boundaries of good taste set by professional designers ... They allow peer acceptance to come higher on a list of what is important than public approval. (Chaplin and Holding, 1998: 8)

This isn't about crediting commercial architecture and lauding its achievements uncritically, but rather about recognising its significance from both a professional point of view and in terms of how it has shaped our experience of the experience society. For many architects 'consumer' is a dirty word, and yet the pressure on the architect to design places that meet consumer needs are intense to say the least. Rem Koolhaas (2008) thus claims that architecture is complicit with a market-driven version of social change in which it is deeply implicated. Koolhaas's argument is that the public, and by implication public space, is totally in thrall to consumption. Or to put this another way, the viability of public space has come to be determined by the ability of that space to entertain the public. From this point of view, although architects would probably be adverse to admitting it, architecture has become about plundering the past, and perhaps more significantly the world of infotainment in order to create 'meaningful' experiences.

In reflecting on Pine and Gilmore's (1999) version of the 'experience economy', Dyckhoff (2017) points out that the role of experience in promoting brands coincided with the shift in Western society from standardisation to one of customisation and individualism. As sophisticated consumers we seek out custom-made solutions, and through these custom-made solutions we feel we can access a better life. The notion that consumption can make our lives better is an interesting one, particularly in the context of architecture, given that it is often based on offering us, as consumers, something we didn't realise we needed. It's in this context that Dyckhoff (2017) discusses the humble bridge, which is no longer about simply crossing a river in order to leave point A and arrive at point B. Rather, bridges, and indeed city promenades, are nowadays made to be looked at as much as looked from. Bridges perform. They are an event, and as such they have to 'enliven space'. Perhaps the best example of a promenade playing a prominent role in how we consume cities is the High Line in Manhattan, New York. Rather than taking the more obvious route of demolishing what had become a derelict privately owned freight viaduct, the Friends of the High Line intervened, championing its experiential credentials and in doing so claiming a kind of collective ownership of the space. The space was in due course turned into an apparently democratic urban promenade. The perceived 'magic' of the space could thus be shared alongside a broader strategy of creating an art and culture district alongside it. Dyckhoff notes that between 2009 and 2014 an incredible 20 million people walked the High Line. But make no mistake, the success of the High Line is inevitably built upon a particular kind of packaging of culture that in turn has created what Dyckhoff calls 'a subculture of voyeurism' along its edges, where ironically a surfeit of toned gym-ready residents appear to reside, thereby adding to the 'experience'. The space is constantly occupied by tourists keen to take in the sensuous enjoyment that the High Line offers them. The magic of the High Line is still there, albeit in a radically altered form, but Dyckhoff (2017: 180) argues that the romance has gone. What it is above all is 'a picturesque landscape for the leisured to promenade through. It is a landscape to consume, with all the senses, but with the sense of sight most of all':

> Once there was a relief from consumerism, spaces you could enter, having paid your taxes, where you were not being sold something. That is no longer an option. As the state has receded from public life, and as public activity has become increasingly contracted out to or

owned by the private sector. So all spaces today come with a business plan. Architecture, after all, has to pay its way.

Public Space, Private Consumption

In June 2018, England progressed further in the World Cup than their abilities might have suggested or perhaps indeed warranted. This created a euphoric public reaction and one that was reproduced in the media by regular images of exultant consumers (I choose that word advisedly) drinking joyously in front of large 'public' TV screens in city centres, and most of all by them recklessly throwing beer into the air on the occasion of England scoring. This was public space as defined by consumption and the unbridled, and apparently uncritical, joy that consumption can bring. But this was also much more than a public expression of communal joy and shared experience: it was the culmination of a process in which the vested interests of a regenerated city defined by consumption pulled together as one (see Koolhaas, 2008). As I noted above, the contemporary city is the product of a whole range of competing pressures and tensions. But what brings these together is a commitment to a vision of a neoliberal or entrepreneurial city (see Harvey, 1989) that simply cannot be challenged as it is so ingrained as to be considered to be 'natural'. Architecture is complicit in a process in the unified neoliberal city that manifests itself as a disunited amalgamation of consumption experiences in which the consumer is inevitably lost:

> The age of spectacle – and the free market that drives it – is still with us today. Though the free market in the gentrified city is hardly free, just open to the highest bidder. What power do any of us have to say yes or no to this building or that? The right to the city has been replaced by the right to buy it. (Dyckhoff, 2017: 351)

Spencer (2016) argues that architecture plays a key role in refashioning human subjects into compliant figures devoted to the market. For Spencer, neoliberalism is a truth game built on the assumption that the market is better equipped to order society than human beings themselves, and that the truths of the market are thus a guarantee of liberty. In this context, the key is flexibility and adaptability: architecture presents itself as a progressive force somewhat lost in the shadowy contours of a neoliberal agenda. But what is interesting here is the way in which Spencer notes that neoliberalism's 'truths' are so well ingrained 'as to substantially shape the conception and experience of selfhood as an essentially productive and adaptive enterprise' (2016: 23). In other words neoliberalism doesn't simply present the economic foundations upon which we construct a social life; it actively determines the shape that social life should take, how it is we conduct ourselves in that context and how we relate to both one another and ourselves. It is in such an environment that the individual subject is obliged to be pliant, productive and competitive. And all this despite the declarations of liberation upon which such expectations are founded.

Spencer goes on to discuss the role of architecture in the so-called 'affective turn'. From this point of view architecture has evolved as a result of the move towards mutability and plurality that has characterised contemporary capitalism. The suggestion is thus that capitalism is no longer the homogenising force we have customarily imagined it to be; rather it is a force for customisation, novelty and difference. The role of spectacular examples of cultural architecture such as the Guggenheim, Bilbao are particularly fascinating in this regard. The conditions in which the gallery exist are tenuous in the sense that so much onus is on the innate ability of the architecture to propel itself. It's in this context that what appears to work in Bilbao may look crass and sensationalist in major cities where the novelty is likely to wear off quicker than you can say 'starchitect' (Ockman, 2004). Storrie (2006) thus suggests that the architect of the Guggenheim, Bilbao, Frank Gehry, has effectively reinvented the museum as a luxurious and untouchable object that is distant from the realities of the place that surrounds it. Architecture then is a key part of the armoury of neoliberalism. The architecturally 'phantasmagoric' is essential in presenting what appears to be a progressive agenda, but one which drowns and camouflages the reality of an institution that props up the status quo while giving it an iconic physical presence.

For Lonsway (2009), the architecture of the experience economy is actually intentionally banal, with the sole intention of framing the consumer experience in such a way as to maximise spend. For him this isn't in any way a radical transformation, but one that constitutes a subtle realignment, best symbolised perhaps by the reinvention of a cup of coffee as a well-crafted experience rather than a simple purchase of a hot drink (see Chapter 8). More importantly, what goes on in that transaction and in so many others like it, is all about generating a brand commitment and repeat acts of consumption. Lonsway seeks to understand experience phenomenologically. From this point of view experience is less something that is produced by marketers to produce economic results and more something of sociological significance worthy of consideration in its own right. In this respect, performance is key and genuine individuality a virtual impossibility given the cast iron grip that the experience economy has on the everyday.

In understanding the above processes, it is important to acknowledge the legacy of the Frankfurt School and the notion that so-called 'mass' consumption penetrates to the extent that what it is that constitutes everything and everywhere is being stretched more and more every single day (see Jameson, 2007). In this light we can perhaps agree with the notion that the contemporary museum constitutes a form of industrialised leisure (Krauss, 1990). But does this process produce anything other than what Augé (1995) describes as non-places, places that cannot be identified as relational, historical or concerned with identity? And is the transformation of such non-places into what Sherry (1998) calls servicescapes – marketing-driven places with a personality that manages to overcome the undifferentiated limitations of the bland landscapes of consumption – really something to which we should aspire? Of course, we can agree with the sentiment that we must listen to the voices of designers and customers in the co-creation of more effective public (and public/private) spaces, but is there a danger that those voices might accidentally conspire to intensify the very trends they were designed to offset? Sternberg (1999) talks about how business manufactures meaning through the infusion of products and experiences that create a market advantage. This process allegedly prompts a kind of self-awareness, so that far from being hoodwinked consumers can make more discerning decisions through environments that increase the consumer's ability to see. At one level this is about designing spaces and places that both entertain and stimulate personal reflection. At another, it is about the ability to prescribe an experience that feels personal. Architects are not passive service providers (Klingmann, 2007). They are not the hapless victims of consumerist excess. They are complicit in the delivery of an ideology that has a permanent effect on the urban landscape, and the longer their profession views consumption with such disdain the more it will remain under its control.

Experiencing Culture

It is of course important not to give the impression that the above process is something that happened overnight as part of some neo-liberal tomfoolery. There is a much broader process going on here, one that has seen the social, and by implication the political, role of culture change considerably over time. The role of architecture in the consumption of culture is particularly telling in this regard insofar as it demonstrates how consumer experience has been appropriated as part of what is essentially a process of instrumental rationality. In this context, the means justify an economic end in which consumer capitalism is all powerful.

As I pointed out in Chapter 1, experience isn't anything new. We have long craved experiences. The world of art is a case in point. Nicholas Serota (2000), former director of the Tate (1988–2017), reflects on a well-established transition in the world of art, namely the shift in curation from 'interpretation' to 'experience'. One characteristic of such a shift is the move towards entering an arts space psychologically rather than just physically, and thereby creating a new kind of relationship between the object and the viewer in which the artist effectively choreographs the experience in order to maximise its effect. In this way, argues Serota, for a long time the gallery visitor has increasingly been expected to chart their own path according to their own particular interests and sensibilities, thus 'redrawing the map of modern art, rather than following a single path laid down by a curator' (2000: 55). Putting to one side the potential spanner in the works of cultural capital, art has long embraced the notion that visitors might go on their own mission of discovery, in which they discover something about themselves *through* art: the incredible impact of installations in the Turbine Hall at Tate Modern, notably Olafur Eliasson's *Weather Project*, being a case in point. The fact that Tate Modern attracts 5.9 million visitors a year is testament to the willingness of key cultural institutions to take risks and to put consumers' needs and wants first, and to perhaps make curatorial compromises in the process (Brown, 2019).

Some authors have argued that cultural spaces are as socially and economically vital today than they have ever been (Thomas, 2016), and this is certainly partly the result of a transformation of culture from something to be learned to something to be experienced. Thomas, for example, goes on to argue that in recent decades, and not least in light of a changing political climate in which culture became a vehicle for social and economic policy, there has been a revitalisation of museums, as places where consumers can discover interests they did not know they had (see Macleod et al., 2018). For Thomas the success of the twenty-first-century museum lies not in the predictability of its offering, but in its ability to provide encounters of curiosity in such a way that they are more than the sum of their storied parts. Museums are places to *be*. And such places reflect the point at which material needs are met, and at which inner experience and the shaping of character become alternative priorities (Von Hantelmann, 2014). This reflects Schulze's (1995) contention that the shift towards inner goals has become the main characteristic of Western society. Culture arguably becomes a means of achieving this, and in doing so its relationship with the past becomes deeply ambiguous insofar as the museum becomes a site for hedonist consumption (Von Hantelmann, 2014).

What I am describing here is a process in which museums, galleries and other cultural forms have become redefined as spaces for entertainment. Museum directors such as Thomas Krens, formerly of New York's Guggenheim Museum, came to see permanent collections as only one element of their offer alongside architecture, exhibitions, shops and restaurants. The invention of museums in such a guise (see also Newhouse, 1998) is arguably tantamount to a theme park with its associated multiple attractions. The gallery is not there solely for the sake of culture, but for the ability of culture to prop up the experience economy. Architecture and design therefore play a key role in providing the spaces in which the performances of the experience society can be played out. They are not innocent bystanders in this process, but active participants. To say that 'The work of building is of no concern to architects because the real work of architecture, as a commodity, is to positively express the abstract structures and concepts of neoliberal capitalism while mystifying its actual conditions of production' (Spencer, 2016: 74) is one thing. More importantly, the ideological power of space as defined through the experience society creates a set of conditions where the consumer, apparently delighted to find him or herself in the process, is made more malleable by the social system that defines them. To paraphrase Hannigan (2005), the pragmatism of architecture lies in the fact that spaces of consumption give consumers what it is they want. They give the consumer the raw materials they need to imagine a life that is reassuringly less chaotic than their own.

One commentator that has sought to get to grips with the flashy, monumental and ostentatious nature of contemporary architecture and the fundamental way it has come to impact our urban spaces is Tom Dyckhoff (2017), whose work I discussed earlier. Dyckhoff examines the fact that in modern art galleries, for example, the building is as much of the creative experience as the art that lies within. This, according to Dyckhoff, reflects a broader trend towards 'white-knuckle' architecture; architecture as fairground ride (e.g. the skywalks of Tianmen Mountain in China's Zhangjiajie National Park) and as picturesque visual experience (e.g. the London Eye). Spaces for entertainment and indeed consumption have gradually adapted to the demands that consumers (assuming a degree of agency in this regard) have of them (see also Lampugnani, 2010). Taking the museum, and specifically the Centre National d'Art et de Culture Georges Pompidou in Paris, as a particularly powerful example, Lampugnani points out that this process is most readily expressed through the consumption of the building itself rather than the art contained within. For Lampugnani, visitors are simply paying homage to what is a 'cultural machine', and as such any notion of any kind of contemplative analysis of art becomes virtually redundant, 'As if they were in a supermarket, visitors are kept in constant motion and forced to consume as they do so' (2010: 251). People consume the experience first and the art second. As far as Lampugnani is concerned there is something significant to lament here given the suggestion that the museum has effectively lost its public purpose.

As the foremost 'luxury branch' of the entertainment industry, culture is simply there to be exploited as a means of stimulating turnover: the artwork is nothing more than a part of a decorative package which often has an iconic building at its heart. In effect, what the emphasis on experience does is make the consumer's taste, rather than the art, its priority. As a result, the consumer is closed off from the unexpected directions that the art might take them. Only that which intensifies their purview, and hence how it is the consumer sees themselves, is relevant. What this means for architecture, design and indeed the creative industries as a whole, is that they become instrumental, so that ironically the commercial baseness that architecture resents is its very raison d'être. But of course, it's important to emphasise that this isn't the architecture industry's 'fault' as such; it is the inevitable consequence of a society that obliges architecture to brush these contradictions under the topographical rug.

A comparable example to that of the Pompidou would be Tate Modern, which could easily be interpreted as little more than a post-industrial spectacle of consumption in which art operates as a means to an experiential end. Built on the site of the regenerated Bankside Power Station in London, Tate Modern has had a monumental social and cultural impact. In one sense this can be said to have been a process of democratisation insofar as the gallery has certainly served to popularise contemporary art. In another it can be said to have undermined it to the extent that it seems to have commodified art to the nth degree. No trip to Tate Modern is complete without a visit to a show of the work of a 'world class' artist (for a considerable extra charge of course), the bookshop-cum-gift shop (like many such museum bookshops it started life with an exhaustive range of books, which were gradually diluted until more profitable souvenirs came to claim centre stage) and the café or restaurant with views to die for, all of which create the impression that the art is in thrall to the experience. From a more positive reading, such spaces provide vibrant social hubs that help to bring urban spaces to life through interactive sociality (Jafari et al., 2013). But even if this were the case, consumption continues to oil the wheels of such interaction.

We might have considered the museums and galleries in the past to be a relief from the obligations of consumerism. This is no longer the case. Museums and galleries depend upon selling popularised versions of what is held within its walls in order to survive (Moss, 2007). And the lines between museums and shops are ever more blurred, as in the archetypal example of the Nike Store, described by Perkins (1995) as a sports retail theatre reveal. Similarly, the Amux Centre in Tokyo is an example of the somewhat indefinable entity of the car museum (in this case representing Toyota), if that is indeed a sufficient marque given the apparently bewildering range of interactive, informative and entertaining environments that this space incorporates. Meanwhile, 'blockbuster' shows that have more in common with the commodified world of the mass media than they do with the rarefied and culturally exclusive world of high art, have become part of the staple diet of urban cosmopolitan culture, raising the suspicion that many galleries are less concerned with what it is they offer and more concerned with how many customers they can get through the door.

Of course, it's easy to be cynical about all this. The fact is that museums and galleries come out of a tradition in which visitors have long been encouraged to pursue their own path of exploration: to experience art through their own eyes. However, such 'freedom' is only possible within a broader process of scripting that underpins the curation process and which could be ultimately described as inherently passive and alienating. Indeed, as Klonk (2009) points out, even the most forthright attempts by artists to make galleries relational social spaces are ultimately empty gestures given that their immersive nature can never be fully embraced by an audience wandering through anxiously on the lookout for the next cultural high. To this end, Klonk (2009) refers to the work of Claire Bishop (2004) in arguing that such efforts 'reproduce the kind of empty and artificial, feel-good atmosphere of a television reality show, with no relation to the divided and fractious societies we live in outside the gallery's wall' (Klonk: 220). A critic might say, of course, that this in itself is connection enough to the experience society in which we live.

Museums have always sought to reassert and reinvent themselves according to the profound socio-economic changes that go on around them (Von Hantelmann, 2014). But of more significance here, notably in Klonk's analysis of art galleries as spaces of experience, is the recognition that as a category, 'experience' has come to straddle the boundaries of the personal and the public. Building upon the legacy of the German philosopher Wilhelm Dilthey, Klonk (2009) argues that galleries have come to focus on developing an experience that is instinctive and intuitive, and that as such it is all about harmonising the visitor's emotional self with that of the display. Of course, not everything from the past can be 're-experienced', and as Kook points out much of this can be consciously choreographed through curation. Neither art nor history are experienced as is, but rather as a product of the narrative through which they are presented (and possibly diluted). It is of course important to remember that this isn't all about the consumption of culture. The artist, for example, might well play a key role in determining what form such consumption might take. The ultimate irony, however, is that the more the artists seeks to challenge or create some kind of alternative to the alleged nightmare of commodification, the more he or she is likely to feed the beast and thereby perpetuate the multiple ways in which capitalism is able to reinvent itself (Krauss, 1990).

Themed Experience

The experience of art and history are one thing, and in their own ways even these elements of twenty-first century culture are highly themed. They are themed in the sense that they can never be presented entirely neutrally, but are always likely to be the product of and contribute to a particular worldview or ideology. This brings to mind a particularly fascinating museum I visited several years ago in China. The museum, which shall remain nameless, depicted the history of battles between China and Japan. The displays were presented as 'fact' but they did not hold back on who was to blame for what. One side, as the English translations put it, were the devil, guilty of unimaginable atrocities, which were portrayed as being even worse when considered against the moral right-thinking intentions of their enemy; the other an uncontested victim. Of course, this is an extreme, and culturally specific example, but what it does illustrate is the potential that culture has for the presentation of a narrative that can blur the lines between fact and fiction. In this context architecture is in service to the seduction of the consumer, and theming is the way it achieves this (Gottdiener, 2001). Theming is thus about the deliberate positioning of products, often devoid of any urban context, as emotional experiences or adventures (Herwig and Holzherr, 2005).

Experience has a key role to play in the blurring of boundaries in many respects, and not least between the mundanity of everyday life and the world of escape that is apparently implied by theming. I discuss one particular manifestation of this, the theme park, in more detail in Chapter 3. But at this stage it is worth considering the broader relationship between experience and theming in the experience society. Theming is a key characteristic of the experience society, the primary characteristic of which is the ability to immerse the consumer within it via architectural, material, performative and technological means (Lukas, 2016). To put this another way, themed environments serve to contain commodified human interaction and involve the investment of symbolic meaning that is conveyed to inhabitants through symbolic motifs. Such motifs can be said to trivialise the built environment in the name of political and economic freedom (Gottdiener, 2001; Fernandez-Galiano, 2005). The prime intention here is to actualise the consumer self. Consumers may satisfy their immediate desires through the experiences such spaces provide, but whether or not this means they have any control over the meaning produced is another question altogether. After all, themed environments are the product of intersecting meaning systems produced, for example, by advertising, economics, the media, politics and even history (Gottdiener, 2001).

Gottdiener goes on to quote the example of the multilevel symbolic environment of Las Vegas as the archetypal themed space. The extremities of Las Vegas have been well documented elsewhere (e.g. Begout, 2003). Suffice it to say, this is a highly immersive space or collection of spaces, but it isn't this way simply to provide entertainment; such immersion is a means by which the consumer's participation in casino gambling can be maximised and, in a way, justified. Gottdiener (2001) thus describes a broader society which is dripping with the symbolism that Las Vegas hints at: 'Increasingly, the problem of capital realisation is solved through the creation of image-driven, themed environments that are attractions themselves but also contain outlets for the sale of commodities. People today consume symbols and environments along with goods and services' (2001: 15). The point that Gottdiener is making is that such spaces are important because they provide the consumer with an added value that a product or service alone cannot provide. They offer a spatial encounter (though not necessarily one with other human beings) in which consumers see themselves at the centre of the experience. But there is a price to pay for all this. Discussing the impact of the private sector on the city in the 1990s, Hannigan (2005) laments the particular demise of public space and the tendency of the so-called 'theme park city' to reproduce a generic sense of placelessness and bland homogeneity. Indeed, the problem is precisely that: experience is effectively the everyday norm. In a sense, themed environments are barely themed at all any more, because theming is so utterly omnipresent. Any tactical means of offsetting the effect of experience are, from this point of view, to be embraced, given that notions of the public are more likely to be subsumed by the dominant narrative that the experience society implies. For Hannigan, the onus on the city as a focus of consumer experience is thus detrimental to any genuine notion of a public culture. Our cities, from this point of view, became less about the people that live in them and more about the creation of fortified and commodified attractions for the visitor. And as Pimlott (2007: 273–4) suggests,

> The automobile-dependent scenes of the Las Vegas Strip with their extreme artificiality and theatrical manipulations, have produced reinforcement for the self-serving tropes of Experience developments … rather than seeking to extend the city and its conditions these developments have constituted aggressive attempts at replacing them. By proposing themselves as surrogates for the city, they have weaned the captive visitor – obliged as usual, to be a consumer – from the desire or need for either the city or its possibilities.

Shopping as Themed Space

For a long time shopping has been at the heart of the urban experience, themed or otherwise. Such prominence has admittedly been increasingly threatened in recent years with the decline of the high street and of bricks-and-mortar retail in general. Many shopping streets in UK towns have effectively become ghost towns dominated by charity and bargain basement shops, and those that are boarded up and unloved. But the visual symbolic appeal of shopping remains in pockets of experiential glee, although it is often discussed as something else. It's no longer the sheer quantity of shopping opportunities that matter, but how those that remain can operate as stage sets for the consumption of self. These days, state-of-the-art reports on retail often draw attention to the fact that good products are not enough to attract customers, but need to operate side by side with immersive experiences that provide the consumer with opportunities to escape (Smithers, 2017). For example, the opening of Westgate Oxford (at a cost of £440 million) was characterised by a clear commitment to 'shoppertainment', in which the store John Lewis collaborated with the Oxford Playhouse theatre. John Lewis committed a fifth of its 11,000 square metres of selling space to services and experiences, from style advice to personalised Christmas decorations. What is more, the John Lewis customer experience is stage managed via an 'experience desk'. This is all about the transition of shopping from a functional activity to a leisure-based one that gives shops a reason to exist in an online age (Wood, 2017).

Not only can visitors to a new shopping mall see and be seen, but they can reinvent themselves in the process. Malls – those whose doors are still open at least – give people what they want, while allowing them to be who they want. Perhaps more importantly, authors such as Hannigan (2005) remind us that this opportunity for reinvention is made available on an unequal basis (not least given the economic downturn and the collapse of the high street in the UK). Not only are such spaces inaccessible to poorer segments of society, but the reproduction of the spectacular city has often led to the removal of particular groups whose presence is deemed detrimental to the process of regeneration. In this context, Kulkarni and Joseph-Lester (2004) refer to the phantasmagorisation of retail architecture, and argue that the commodity is now so inscribed on space that it has served to create a new kind of reality. The irony here is that such space purports to bring with it infinite qualities and possibilities so that the spectator's imagination is allegedly liberated by and collapsed into the spectacle:

> Shoppers are subjected to the interests of the store and relinquish a degree of their spatial autonomy. In return, the space engages the imagination in a way that extends the physical limits of the building. Caught within this fantasyscape, consumers forget any rational motive for shopping and enter the phantasmagoria of spectacle and disorientation … This space of delirium is offered to the shopper as a site of freedom, a freedom that must, however, move in step with the demands and motivations of capital … This fantasyscape allows the imagination to extend experience into a terrain that is always in motion. (2004: 14–26)

Shopping has become an increasingly subtle and sophisticated experience to the extent that the city has itself effectively become, 'a shopping Mecca of unparalleled entertainment experience' (Moss, 2007: 115), or indeed the ultimate shopping mall. Taking this to the extreme, shopping has become the defining activity of public life (Sze Tsung Leong, 2011). The shopping experience is therefore, in a sense, magical: it provides the consumer with a liminal space of self-discovery, the ability to move from one themed space to another, and the fact that this experience is as much imaginary as it is physical is the reason for its power over the popular imagination. Pimlott (2007) identifies what he describes as a process of 'instantaneous' city making which has emerged as the product of the merging of two typologies – the shopping mall (representing urban space) and the Las Vegas casino (representing urban vitality) – so that the creation of retail environments or experiences becomes the primary focus. For Pimlott there is indeed a strong manipulative element to all this, notably through the enthusiastic consumption of such zones after the Second World War. Such spaces were deliberately congested so as to create an overwhelming experience that replicated the busy city streets of the pre-war years. Such a collage-like representation of city chaos has now become a way of life to the extent that Jerde's Freemont Street Experience and Universal City Walk LA present versions of a world in which it is natural to feel that we are simply performing on the city stage. Jerde effectively orchestrates experience, promoting what Klingmann (2007) describes as an 'intense heterogeneity' in which symbols and themes are set out on a deliberate collision course so that the potential for the application of meaning is boundless. This environment may be staged, but it has an emotional impact on its audience that is real (Klingmann, 2007).

The above process poses a whole raft of ideological questions. What is being described is a city that comes to life through how the consumer engages with consumer capitalism via the imagination. This is perhaps best summed up in the above-mentioned architecture of Jon Jerde, whose key projects are often seen to be archetypes of an experiential architecture in which the city is envisioned as a mode of entertainment (e.g. New York-New York Casino in Las Vegas). But what's particularly crucial here, and what underpins this book as a whole, is the suggestion that the consumer is no longer being tricked or disempowered by such ideological forces. As Kulkarni and Joseph-Lester (2004: 35) put it, 'We now willingly relinquish our control over the space that surrounds us. As a means to experience the fantasy of the unknown. The paradox is that entertainment is both the site of freedom and disempowerment; it simultaneously articulates a fantasy of excess and a reality of manipulation.' Consumption in an experience society may be more intense, but so is the ideology that underpins it.

Conclusion

The experience society has created spaces and places for consumption in which the potential for control, magnified by the access to our own information that the world of consumption has, is magnified. On the back of this, neoliberalism is able to use the mirage of spontaneity and self-production for its own devious ends. Architecture is thus deemed by Spencer (2016) to be compliant with the neoliberal agenda. The ideals of the society in which we live, those of environmental awareness, of a world yet to be protected by the market, and one that is apparently devoid of individual spontaneity, is helpless insofar as human nature is reproduced through the guise of neoliberalism so that exiting technologies of the self are reinvented to its own ends. This argument is significant in a broader theoretical context. As Jameson (2007) points out, it reinforces the argument that members of the Frankfurt School made regarding the totalising nature of the logic of late capitalism as expressed through consumer culture and its ability to penetrate everywhere and everything. For many this draws a picture of the passive consumer hungrily looking for fulfilment through the experiences that the city and its design can provide. For authors like Dyckhoff (2017), what he calls the city of spectacle is bereft of freedom. On the surface it may provide a prettier city, but it is also an overpriced city and as such one that most of us can barely dream of actually living in. The city has in the end become something to admire from afar, something to consume rather than a place in which human beings can thrive.

The ideological process that underpins all this is one in which, as authors such as Dyckhoff (2017) and Klein have suggested, branding has become life itself. The world of experience that has resulted from the world of brands that surrounds us is not on the periphery anymore. It hasn't been for a long time. Regardless of the economic conditions we find ourselves in, our very being is structured by the values that the experience society creates for us. And as I said at the beginning of this chapter, the physical spaces that we live through are not neutral; they breathe life into the status quo and they keep breathing. More importantly, the experiences that define our relationship with the city of consumption and how they help us to imagine ourselves in the process create a dependency that represents the most extreme physical manifestation of consumerist ideology imaginable. The spaces and places that the designers of experience create for us are not accidental but are the product of a particular instrumental logic (Pimlott, 2007). They create a naturalised, disenchanted world of fragmentary encounters in which consumption serves the capitalist cause, while prioritising the seductive ecstasies of space at the expense of the calmer, more rudimentary raptures of places undiscovered.

7

The Spectacle of Sport

The meaning of sport has been radically transformed over the past 20 to 30 years. In one sense this is all about injecting sport with added value; to make it worth more on the market than the sum of its individual parts. Or to put it another way, the lines between sport and entertainment have become increasingly blurred (Westerbeek and Smith, 2003). This is a process that has the reinvention of consumption as experience at its very core. If you were going to put an exact date on this transformation it might well be 20 February 1992, when the old First Division of English football broke away from the Second Division of English football to create the Premiership and latterly the Premier League. Sport had, virtually overnight, became a fulcrum for experiential consumption in such a way that the personalised meaning that appeared to underpin what it meant to be a supporter would never be the same again. By looking in more depth at sport as, arguably, the spectacular shining beacon of the experience society we can further unravel the paradoxes of that society, while also reflecting upon consumer capitalism's ability to give with one experience and yet take away with another.

Sport Commodified

There has been a long tradition of understanding the production of sport through the lens of Marxism, yet more recently sport has remained a relatively underdeveloped area of exploration when you consider Marxist scholarship on popular culture more generally (Carrington and McDonald, 2008). The theme of this latter body of work has tended to be concerned with the aggressive exploitation of culture as a means of capital accumulation (Andrews, 2008). From this point of view the history of sport in this period has been one of commercialisation, corporatisation and spectacularisation. The first two notions centre on the exploitation of a practice for commercial gain and the structuring of

sport on the basis of the profit motive, and it is upon these foundations that sport grew as an entertainment-driven experience. Kellner
(2003) argues that sport 'emerged as the correlative to a society that is
replacing manual labour with automation and machines, and requires
consumption and appropriation of spectacles to reproduce consumer
society' (Kellner, 2003: 66). Thus sport can be said to provide a means
by which individuals learn the values of a competitively aspirational,
success-driven society. For Kellner, spectator sports proactively mobilise
spectators around sport as a celebration of sporting virtue and achievement. This is a transition from what used to be, in the industrial era,
all about labour and production, but more significantly perhaps about
the strength of working collectively towards a common goal. Sports
were drenched in capitalist virtues of competition and in notions of
professionalism. Sport provided a means of assimilating people into the
values being upheld by society as a whole. For some, sport is essentially
a class practice deserved of being 'smashed' like the capitalist system
itself (Brohm, 1978). The role of sport from this Marxist position is to
contain aggressive desires and to neutralise them as a means of protect-
ing the future of capitalism. Another way of putting this might be to say
that sport acts as a kind of catharsis machine that absorbs the stresses
of the class struggle in a new, codified form of violence. And in doing
so, it channels the energies of the masses into a position where they are
propping up the established order (Perelman, 2012).

The question mark hanging over the above analysis centres on
whether or not such an approach underestimates the ability of consumers to interpret and navigate the complex set of interrelationships that
exist between structures of social control and experience (Miles, 1998).
Is the Marxist critique of sport simply one-dimensional (Whannel,
1992)? What we can be sure of is that sport has always been subject
to a process of change, and that these changes always tend to imply an
act of consumption (Crawford, 2004). In one sense, the emergence of
sport as a fully fledged commodity simply reflects broader economic
and geographical changes and global transformations in the circula-
tion and reception of images (Horne, 2006). But what's most important
here, as Horne (2006) notes, is the point that however much this world
appears to have opened up the market, it has not managed to simultaneously liberate the consumer. Ultimately, purchasing power is very
different to market power (see also Coates, 1995). As Horne (2006)

argues, consumption effectively operates *in the service of* production. What this tells us is that however much the consumption of sport, and consumption more generally, serves our sense of who we are, it does so for an ancillary reason. The experience society is founded on the drive to perpetuate this principle; to perpetuate a world in which the individual consumer feels alive at the cost of a life inevitably lived at the behest of consumer capitalism.

In the post-industrial era sport has transitioned hand in hand with a society that is now so thoroughly automated and media driven that we can, not unreasonably, go as far as to describe the Premier League as a media rights selling organisation 'that happens to provide 20 clubs with a platform, a referee and a ball' (Clegg and Robinson, 2018). Sport is a commercial beast. Approaching £5 billion was committed to Premier League clubs for live broadcasting rights from 2019 to 2022. But what is perhaps more interesting, and more profound as far as the evolution of an experience society is concerned, is that sport allows fans to partake in something that is bigger than they are. Its communal nature and the shared spirit and joys, as well as the sorrows and pains, that fans can share, mean that it can provide what is a uniquely fervent and passionate audience, but one that is also in danger of being exploited for that very reason (Conn, 2018; Kellner, 2003).

It is in this spirit that we can consider sport to be a bona fide culture industry in which a product is manufactured for the pleasure of a mass audience (see Adorno, 1991a). This is, of course, part of a longer-term process in which symbolic value has come to the fore as a means of stimulating consumer demand and of propelling consumer capitalism as it colonises new markets. In short, as authors such as Jameson (1991) have noted, late capitalism has reinvented itself as a mode of cultural production, within which the boundaries between the economic and the cultural have become increasingly hazy. The key lies perhaps in an understanding of the commercial interconnectedness of sport which has been aggressively commercialised to the extent that we can now barely imagine it outside its commercial form. For example, Porat (2012) talks about the gradual commodification of football and how the community roots of football in Israel were gradually eroded by a process of marketisation that underpinned social change in the 1990s. Again, this is all about commodification, given that 'capitalism's ultimate ongoing goal is to turn virtually everything into a commodity – labour power included – because when something is commodified, it is assigned an exchange value and then succumbs to the logic of the market' (2012: 443). Such logic is inevitable and only varies depending on the political and cultural context in which it arises. In Israel, the rise of privatisation was always going to have an impact on the emergence of professional sport, which was obliged to respond to the economic changes going on around it, if only to survive. Marx, of course, suggests that commodification can only be fully understood in the context of a broader process of social change; it's how capitalism does this and through which mechanisms that is of interest here, when we think about the nature of the shift to the experience society.

But what's really missing is what all this means for the individual consumer and how he or she is brought within the capitalist 'family'. What is so interesting about sport in a so-called late capitalist society is the process whereby big business has come to play an increasingly influential role in the running and organisation of sport (Giulianotti, 2002). This is a relationship fuelled by the mass media (Crawford, 2004). It is almost unthinkable now to note that the English Football Association resisted live football coverage (with the exception of the FA Cup Final) right up until 1983. Nowadays, you could almost say that football barely exists, certainly in the UK, outside the confines of Sky Sports, BT Sport, the BBC and ITV. It is its own media reality. Sky Sports alone shows 126 live Premier League matches per season while Amazon has broken the Sky Sports/BT Sport monopoly by securing the rights to 20 games of its own. The point is that the relationship between football and the media long ago took the onus away from the immediacy of the match-day experience and made that experience increasingly abstract and tempered by a media representation of what sport *should* be. Football sits at the very fulcrum of globalisation and is the living realisation of a capitalism that thrives on the breathless, the 'flash and glitter of the instantaneous' and the promise of quick financial reward (Perelman, 2012: 77). It is the media that is tasked with delivering the superior product of football as represented by the Premier League and the European Champions League. The total revenue of clubs in Europe's top divisions has tripled since 2000 (MacInnes, 2018). Meanwhile, it has even been argued that sport and the media have been amalgamated in a kind of 'reformatting' of the world, so that 'the difference between living reality and its representation is permanently blurred' (Perelman, 2012: 94).

Sporting Celebrity

Sports stars are the grease that keeps the wheels of sporting enterprise turning. So what influence do celebrities have on how we consume, and what does our consumption say about us? Cashmore (2014) argues that by attaching the names of celebrities to particular products those products are given a degree of personality that wouldn't otherwise be available to them. For example, a consumer might not admire a particular mobile phone company or a brand of shampoo, but by attaching a celebrity to such a product his or her admiration for that celebrity is transferred to the product. We as consumers subconsciously appropriate the attributes associated with celebrities: they make us feel good about ourselves. The contemporary media-driven world is utterly preoccupied with imagery. Sport doesn't exist in a vacuum and innovation in sport reflects and indeed contributes to the way in which society evolves and vice versa (Smart, 2005). A good example of that is the recent development of on-court/pitch technology to support decisions in sports including tennis and football. Such developments simply would not have happened without television. But they fundamentally affect the product and, for better or worse, they change the natural rhythms of the game.

Returning to the question of sporting celebrity, it might be argued that the process we are witnessing in fact represents a shift from that of lionising a sporting hero to putting the celebrity on a pedestal (and often back down again) insofar as while the former are somehow 'natural' the latter are manufactured; that the celebrities we admire today are, arguably, somehow less 'authentic' than they were in the past. The English footballer Raheem Sterling is an interesting case in point. Sterling is a sporting celebrity that has gone through a number of media-driven stages, from a player of immense potential at Liverpool, to someone who was vilified by many England supporters for not having an end product, as a potential poster boy for the anti-racism movement and at the time of writing, a complex figure who's physical aggression towards an England teammate culminated in him being dropped for an important Euro 2019 qualification match. Sterling, a Manchester City and England forward, is an intriguing case insofar as the media has constructed a narrative around him, and that narrative has effectively become the truth. Whether commenting two or three times on racism in sport qualifies him as a fully fledged authority on the subject is by the by. If the media say he is then he is.

The ultimate global sports celebrity of all time is of course Michael Jordan. Jordan was a ridiculously skilful NBA superstar. But perhaps more significant than that is the fact that in June 1998 *Fortune* magazine estimated that during the course of his career he generated an incredible $110 billion of added value while simultaneously fetishising victory and success. The strapline 'Just Do It' signified that anybody was capable, just like Jordan, of achieving what it is they wanted to achieve and this in itself was commercial gold dust (Kellner, 2003). The emergence of Michael Jordan is a measure of the rise of sport as experience: it is testament to the ability of sport to not only provide role models, but to create the mindspace and the associated products for consumption (e.g. training shoes) that allow consumers to feel that they are part of it. But this only tells half the story. Hughson et al. (2005) have argued that when young sport stars are sucked into the vacuum of celebrity they are, more worryingly, obliged to become role models and as such are 'burdened with a presumed greater moral obligation' (2005: 109). It is in this way, argues Hughson, that sport is carefully attuned to wider social norms and expectations, and not least the furore that surrounds the morals and actions of young professional footballers (Blackshaw and Crabbe, 2004), so that even rape and sexual deviance is consumed culturally and in such a way that it feeds the experience culture that defines us. The world of celebrity becomes 'our world': we see the world through the lens that the mass media obliges us to consume. As such,

> the 'crisis' enveloping English professional football ... reveals not the horrors of rape or any genuine, universal moral repugnance but rather the presentation of rape and sexual deviance as a titillating performance for widespread public consumption. There is no 'moral panic' only a soap opera scandal. We are faced with a staged presentation of morality, with its own twists and turns, subplots and spin, to which we are all party and which gives us license to 'safely' consume the 'deviance' of others. (Blackshaw and Crabbe, 2004: 178)

The question mark here concerns what it is consumers are actually consuming in an experience society. The media certainly dilutes and personalises the footballing experience, but there is something fascinating about the cocoon that the sporting experience provides. There is a degree of complicity going on: even deviance is performed so that the worst examples of human behaviour are glamourised and commodified (Blackshaw and Crabbe, 2004). Consumers are complicit insofar as they allow this to happen and they seek out the experience, possibly to reflect upon, or indeed deflect from, the mundane normality of their own lifestyles. But more than this, sport becomes the consumer's world, not least in the context of social media (see Chapter 5), which gives everyone licence to say and share what it is they feel about the latest media-driven sporting intrigue, regardless of its veracity. An experience society is a society in which no individual's opinion is more valid than any other's. The impact of the media is such that the consumer is glorified: liberated and buttressed by a world outside of their experience, but one that allows them to feel they do matter, why diverting them from what really does. But what is it about sport that makes this happen?

Mediating the Sporting Spectacular

Top-level sport is a truly global institution. Manchester United alone boast an estimated 659 million supporters worldwide. Clearly, only a very small proportion of these fans ever actually get to see their under-performing team in the flesh. The version of United that most supporters engage with is a form of spectacular consumption that can be accessed immediately in the stadium, or arguably even more spectacularly from the comfort of the fan's own home. It is therefore perhaps most informative to think of sport as a spectacle.

The most beneficial theoretical means of doing so is through the work of Guy Debord (1995), whom I discussed in some detail in Chapter 2. Debord sees the spectacle as a metaphorical key by which we can understand consumer society: the notion of the spectacle as ideology. Debord is interested in the process by which mass media technology is visually deceptive, and how mediated images sit at the centre of an economic sphere while serving to construct an objective reality. The relationship between business, sport and television creates a heady mix; an entertainment high which, as Andrews (2006) puts it, incorporates tropes across the breadth of human experience (such as triumph/tragedy/ success and failure/heroism/villainy) while simultaneously serving to humanise and personalise the whole experience in what is a phantasmagoria of sensory gratification. The society of the spectacle, according to Debord, creates a set of conditions in which the commodity is all powerful in constructing a world in its own guise.

What is so intriguing about the sporting experience is precisely the above: the way that such a process feeds a version of selfhood in a particularly verified fashion. This isn't a simple case of supporters going to a match or viewing that match on television. Much of what we understand the Premier League to be is the product of a media discourse which sieves how we engage with the sport we love, the effect being to intensify or exaggerate the nature of the connection we have. As such, Blackshaw and Crabbe (2004) argue that what fans consume via their sofas is effectively *designed* for *their* consumption. The word *their* is particularly important here, it is through the range of available media-driven options the individual gets to consume the sporting spectacle in the way he or she sees fit. Consumers are drawn into sport by the exaggerated version of the spectacle that is provided for them. This mediated version of sport is thrilling, exciting and as such provides the fan with a buzz that may otherwise not be accessible through the everyday. Fans do not consume sport in this sense, they experience it.

Long ago the Frankfurt School identified a transition in which what we consumed provided a means of pacification, something that Manzenreiter (2006) also explores in his work, pointing out that 'the fetishism of the commodity prevents the subject from satisfying her/his actual human needs; it destroys any collective form of society by individualizing the subjects who are nonetheless forced into uniformities of action and thought for the purposes of stabilising structures of domination' (Manzenreiter, 2006: 153). Under the all-encompassing guise of the spectacle the consumer becomes the centrepiece of their own script. The performativity that the spectacle implies puts the individual front and centre. The clichéd TV image of supporters watching forlorn as their downtrodden team look like losing an important game, and yet rematerialise exulted when they catch themselves appearing on the big screen in the stadium, speaks to a process that tells us everything we need to know. In this moment the experience is no longer of a sporting event but of a process in which the self is located via the event. This is all underpinned by the frailties that underpin human existence and by how easily such frailties can be used and exploited for the so-called economic good. But the point here is that the consumer is more complicit in this

THE SPECTACLE OF SPORT

process than he or she may have been in the past. He or she is fully aware of the power that the media possesses and he or she appears to embrace that power.

In many ways, late capitalist societies are increasingly defined by their relationship to spectacle and the spectacular to the extent that the distinction between the 'performers' and their audience is increasingly blurred (Crawford, 2004). Crawford describes the performance of supporters as a kind of controlled and disciplined carnival which encourages particular forms of commodified behaviour (e.g. singing and chanting) while discouraging others (e.g. violent behaviour or drunkenness). Many critics have condemned any notion of spectacle as being vague and one-dimensional (see Horne and Whannel, 2012). This kind of a criticism is largely founded on the suggestion that such claims amount to a lazy, often leftist condemnation of complex phenomena. Horne and Whannel (2012) question the carnivalesque nature of the sporting spectacle, and the degree to which it makes a genuine difference outside its immediate confines.

For Bakhtin (1984), the carnival constitutes an alternative social space characterised by freedom, equality and abundance. Everyone is equal in the space of the carnival which is utopian insofar as it provides a moment of escape, of freedom from the everyday: at this moment the individual embraces the moment and just the moment; life is encapsulated in the immediacy of festivity. This has a significant psychological dimension, given that the carnival spirit provides a means of freeing human consciousness and opening up human potential. It is the carnivalesque that opens up a pathway for human imagination. As Robinson (2011) suggests in discussing the notion of the carnival, the golden age it garners is lived, not through inner thought or experience, but more profoundly by the whole person, in thought and body. But the carnival that Bakhtin describes replaces the orthodoxy of a dominant ideology. It is antithetical to sterile norms. As Robinson puts it, 'In carnival, everything is rendered ever-changing, playful and undefined. Hierarchies are overturned through inversions, debasements and profanations, performed by normally silenced voices and energies' (Robinson, 2019). The carnival makes us feel alive. But perhaps it conceals as much as it reveals.

What is being described here appears to be the diametrical opposite to the carnival that sport, and the broader experience society, presents to us today. To an extent the live experience of the sporting spectacle offers some sense of fantasy and social frisson, through, for example, the tensions that exist between opposing fans. Such an aura *is* realised through the sense of communal power, and indeed the sense of belonging that the crowd provides. To give you an example, as a Nottingham Forest supporter, at least from a distance, I get to see my team play a couple of times a season. On one such occasion 'we' were playing our local rivalries, whose name I find it difficult to commit to paper. The said team were 2–1 up until the last minute when Forest forced an equaliser. The stadium erupted. This was a moment of extreme intensity; of personal and communal outpouring. A young Forest supporter stood next to me, around about eight years of age. I picked him up and threw him into the air as the crowd fused in its joy. In normal circumstances such an act would have been unacceptable, but at that moment it was just part of the communal experience: an instinctive response to a moment of sheer magic. It's in this respect that Giulianotti (2011) talks about the intense experience that a live football match can offer: transfixing, flow-like and all-embracing. Or perhaps consider what's going on here as part of a process in which the everyday is being aestheticised. Consumers are perhaps obliged to reflect on the world around them as a performance put on for their sake, and herein lies the intensity (Abercrombie and Longhurst, 1998). Back in 1992 John Fiske argued that fans were semantically productive, that their experience is about meaning-making and the sharing of meaning with fellow fans. He or she produces, and perhaps constructs, a sense of identity along the way. And yet he or she inevitably does so in ways which buttress the market in the process. Consumer capitalism revitalises the self, but in doing so it revitalises consumer capitalism.

Football may well remain the most purely commodified of sports. How we consume football is not untempered. Our experience of football is just like any other sport, yet magnified to the extreme. Such experience can only be understood as part of a broader set of circumstances in which the sporting public are tightly controlled. As Giulianotti (2011) suggests, the football experience continues to be highly securitised, sanitised even, not least in Britain since the Taylor Report in 1990 which introduced all-seater stadiums in the aftermath of the Hillsborough disaster of 1989 in which 96 Liverpool supporters were fatally injured. This, alongside a broader process in which the footballing commodity was further, and understandably, packaged to appeal to middle-class and cosmopolitan tastes, created a 'product' that if anything has diluted the public spectacle and undermined the flow of 'fantasy lives' that the experience offers. We consume football as individuals passionate about the sport and the club we support. But this passion represents little more than a palette upon which we can both escape from ourselves and yet discover a transitory version of ourselves at one and the same time.

The Narcissistic Spectacular

Perhaps we would be best exercised at this stage to consider the specific potential of sport and its broader relationship to social change. One of the most intriguing approaches to the transformation of sport is that of Christopher Lasch (1979) in his book *The Culture of Narcissism*. Lasch discusses the development of a discourse emerging around sport in the second half of the twentieth century in which work became abstract and interpersonal, a kind of protective shell of self-imprisonment. Sport, in contrast, offered a less rationalised arena that recreates a kind of child-hood exuberance and escape, or at least it did until the onset of the post-industrial world. 'Commercialization has turned play into work, subordinated the athlete's pleasure to the spectator's, and reduced the spectator himself to a state of vegetative passivity – the very antithesis of the health and vigour sport ideally promotes' (Lasch, 1979: 103). For Lasch there is something very important going on here. Sport reaffirms a set of common cultural values, while in other respects actively undermining them. He thus describes a contamination of standards in which sports were being seduced by the limitless promises of television, even 40 years ago, while compromising themselves in the process: speed snooker and the selling of Test Cricket rights to Sky TV immediately come to mind in this regard. Lasch describes sports spectators in this context as 'sensation hungry'. The example Lasch gives of ice hockey is a further case in point: the drama of violence has become the focal point for its consumption. Sport thus becomes a product of its own spectacular making. And for this reason the sporting spectacle should not be taken for granted:

Today that the world is conceived as a series of spectacles is to say that it is treated as something to be attended to. No longer can people,

objects or events be simply taken for granted; they are instead constituted as performances which command audiences. At the same time
as the world is full of performing entities, the characteristic personality structure of contemporary societies is narcissistic ... individuals
see themselves as performers in front of an imagined audience. (Abercrombie and Longhurst, 1998: 97)

One particularly graphic example of this is the so-called lineal heavy-
weight boxing champion of the world (at the time of writing), Tyson
Fury. Fury has lived a colourful life, much of which he has described as
a performance. Appearing as Batman at press conferences, trash-talking
his opponents, making controversial statements and most recently of
all stepping into the world of 'sports entertainment' by 'fighting' (such
events are fixed) rival Braun Strowman in a WWE wrestling bout in
Saudi Arabia, Fury has also talked about the impact of his ambitions
on his mental health. Resplendent in Stars and Stripes shorts in his last
boxing bout, and entering the wrestling ring wearing traditional Arabic
dress, Fury is a deliberate, and arguably somewhat cynical, crowd
pleaser. He and the people around him are self-consciously constructing
a sporting carnival that goes one step further than simply putting on an
exciting sporting event. What Fury does is invest such events with additional meaning, thereby enhancing the range within which the audience
can attach their own. In other words, Fury operates as an archetype of
the experience society by persuading his audience that they can relate to
him, and his personal struggles, in a very human way. The commodity
Fury presents is a spectacular one, carnivalesque even, but the consumer
takes that carnival and makes it his or her own.

Cricket and the Power of the Spectacle

Let us consider the process of 'spectacularisation' in a little more depth.
A particularly good example of its effect can be found in cricket, which
has in recent years been reinvented by the re-emergence of the Indian
Premier League (IPL) and of Twenty20 cricket more generally. The IPL,
the bedazzling shining light of the reinvention of cricket, was founded in
2007 and represents the polar opposite of what was hitherto regarded as
the gold standard of the sport, namely the Test Match (which is stretched
over five days and four innings and often ends in a draw). The new

IPL format consists of two teams, each of which bats for a compressed number of 20 overs in a rapid-fire series of contests that takes place over a two-month period between April and May. The excitement is intensified by an auction process that allows teams to parachute players in for the duration. The sheer commercial power of the IPL is illustrated by the fact that in 2015 it contributed US$182 million to India's gross domestic product. The IPL is a television phenomenon with a cumulative reach of 295 million viewers in India alone. In March 2009 the IPL signed a ten-year, US$1.8 billion broadcast deal with Multi Screen Media, while its current brand is estimated at US$6.3 billion (Khondker and Robertson, 2018).

What is most interesting about the IPL is how it has so brazenly gone about reinventing cricket. Twenty20 is a game of speed and power that's all about hitting a cricket ball hard and scoring runs quickly which, as Khondker and Robertson (2018) point out, is in stark contrast to the gentlemanly elegance associated with the cricket of the past. This is cricket as pure commodification, and according to its emergence reflects the broader normalisation of consumption in Indian society. From this point of view IPL is all about the imposition of a market logic on the game through revenues accumulated by teams, or rather 'franchises', that have little meaning other than as oracles for the maximisation of profit, not just through the products attached to the IPL but by the consumption of the sport itself. This is about spectacularising cricket, as well as about inviting the new Indian middle classes (an estimated 600 million of them) into exploring their consumer self in a new guise: sport as entertainment (Khondker and Robertson, 2018).

Khondker and Robertson (2018) thus describe the IPL as being 'deterritorialized', not least as its existence clearly depends more on its televisual impact than on its physical location. In this sense the crowd is nothing more than part of the spectacle: a means to a spectacular end with balls being smashed out of the stadium and fireworks being set off in time to the metaphorical fireworks going on as part of the game. What does this tell us about the way in which consumption is changing? Does it simply mean that to strip sport of its underlying tribal loyalties is to rid it of its heart, or is there something more complicated going on? It could be argued that the IPL demonstrates how the experience the contemporary sporting product offers is not quite as individualised as it might appear. And yet its spectacular nature is no doubt affecting its audience in a way that is somewhat different to the tribal loyalties usually associated with the sporting enterprise. This brings us back to the work of Lasch (1979), who describes a process in which sport has come to be presented for profit's sake. But this in turn has a profound psycho-social impact:

> No one denies the desirability of participation in sports – not because it builds strong bodies but because it brings joy and delight. It is by watching those who have mastered a sport, however, that we derive standards against which to measure ourselves. By entering imaginatively into their world, we experience in heightened form the pain of defeat and the triumph of persistence in the face of adversity. An athletic performance, like other performances, calls up a rich train of associations and fantasies, sharpening unconscious perceptions of life. Spectatorship is no more 'passive' than daydreaming, provided the performance is of such quality that it elicits an emotional response. (1979: 107)

What is key here is the emotional response that sports like cricket and the IPL can engender: they intensify the fantasyland that sport allows us to create for ourselves. For Lasch the beauty of sport lies in the opportunity for the consumer to escape into the make-believe it provides. The irony is that the very thing that Lasch appears to lament – the supposed undermining of the emotional heart of the sporting experience – is the very thing that is being exploited by the recent reinvention of sport as experience. Lasch does point out that sport has degenerated into spectacle. The success and meaningfulness of sport lies, from this point of view, in how sport, which is in the end a relatively trivial activity, has been endowed with meaning that results in it becoming a representation of life more broadly. This constitutes what Lasch describes as an 'attack on illusion': the illusion of reality that sport at its beautiful best is capable of creating.

But the processes that Lasch describes has morphed into something much more telling than he could ever have anticipated, insofar as it now appears to combine a notion of sport as entertainment with the very fantasy that history seemed to suggest this process would undermine. The power of the experience society is, to borrow from Kipling's oft-quoted poem and as inscribed over the entryway to the Centre Court at Wimbledon: 'If you can meet with Triumph and Disaster, and treat those two imposters just the same'. Fantasy and spectacle are no longer in conflict, yet they have been unified in such a way that the consumer has been rendered powerful and yet powerless at one and the same time. The spectacle has become individualised in such a way that the quality of consolation that sport offers is subsumed into the process of ideological homogenisation. This is testament to the never-ending pragmatism of consumer capitalism and its ability to reinvent itself, in this case as simultaneously distant and yet personal: but not *too* personal. Entertainment for and of the self.

Conclusion

The above argument takes us back to Kellner's (2003) notion that sports fans become part of something in excess of their own self. This process is inevitably intensified in a world in which sport is defined through the media. The media constructs a state of affairs in which the pathway to selfhood appears to be individualised and yet which is increasingly constrained. The choice to watch all your club's matches on satellite television or perhaps online does not serve to liberate the consumer, it ties you to a tightly confined version of who you are. The supporter commits to his or her club, but in doing so commits to a lesser version of him or herself in the sense that he or she is constructed from a less diverse palette. In driving the above process the media is not necessarily more powerful than it was, say 20 years ago, but it is so much more subtle and all-embracing and as such it is able to tailor the individual's sporting consumption in such a way that how they experience what they consume becomes a more essential part of who it is they are.

Experience obliges the sports fans to filter a sense of themselves through a version of sport and belonging which they are convinced is of their own making. Fantasy sports leagues are a case in point insofar as they effectively dehumanise athletes and put consumers/fans at the forefront of the consumption experience (Ploeg, 2017). However, the vast menu from which they appear to choose actually constitutes a capitulation of the self. It certainly *feels* like the identity one can muster through sporting loyalty is a profound one, and in a sense it is, but ultimately such an identity is like a tsunami washing away all other possibilities so that one of the only ways the individual sports fan can see themselves is through the prism that their experience of their pseudo-relationship to their club or sporting hero provides. 'In sports events, fans become part of something greater than themselves, the participation provides meaning and significance, and a higher communal self, fused with the multitude of believers and the spirit of joy in triumph and suffering in tribulation' (Kellner, 2003: 69). A key question centres on the extent to which the consumer can actively resist the irresistible, or if he or she might not even try. The notion of passivity is an interesting one and puts the spotlight on how and why people consume the sporting spectacular. Is the consumer experience of sport a 'passive' one? Is the sense that fans can individualise their sporting experiences purely illusory? In April 2019 Tottenham Hotspur Football Club opened up their state-of-the-art stadium to general media and public acclaim. The key selling point of the stadium was that it offered spectators not just a place to watch their team play, but 'one of the finest spectator experiences in the world': a place you would stay in before and after the match itself. The stadium includes its own micro-brewery, an in-house bakery, USB ports in seats, and the longest bar in the UK. A place you would want to hang out (and spend) in. But this isn't a space you can make your own, or is it?

Sport takes many forms. In this chapter, I have mainly focused on the sporting spectacle: sports to be consumed from afar or at least second hand. The kinds of processes I have been describing are intensified by the mirroring of sporting physicality in everyday life, not least through, for example, the personalisation of fitness and how someone constructs their sense of self through the sporting body (see Chapters 2 and 3). This too has significant psychological implications. For the cultural commentator Mark Greif (2017) the consumption of the gym is in part a biological calling, a process of biological self-regulation, 'But the true payoff of a society that chooses not to make private freedoms and private leisures its main substance has been much more unexpected. This payoff is a set of forms of bodily self-regulation that drags the last vestiges of biological life into the light as a social attraction' (2017: 6). In one sense the gym is a more solitary experience than supporting a club or team, but being in a gym or even running in the street are not solitary acts at all in the sense that they represent the individual consumer making a commitment to notions of self that reside in the body; a body to be consumed by others. This process is deeply ironic insofar as it commits the individual to a surface-driven conception of the self. The more he or she works on the body the more he or she's body is replicated and the more he or she reproduces social ideals. The process that Greif describes is highly pertinent to my discussion of experience. Consumers of fitness make a public spectacle of themselves. The privacy of personal health is made available as a spectacle for everybody to consume. In that process any quest for liberation and healthy superiority is inevitably lost, for what the individual becomes is nothing more profound than the experience through which he or she defines him or herself.

In considering the changing nature of the relationship between sport and identity, it is also important to remember the equally significant rise of lifestyle sports and their role in the construction of self. Such sports including surfing, skateboarding, snowboarding and windsurfing, all of which are as subject to the processes of commercialisation as any of the other sports mentioned above. For example, Beal and Wilson (2004) discuss the evolution of skateboarding as a mass product. They note that the legitimisation of skateboarding as a sport gives skateboarders considerable pleasure and material opportunities for personalisation. Skateboarding, in particular, and especially for men, is all about risk and the display of rugged individualism which reproduce traditional notions of masculinity. What consumption does is to effectively camouflage this process, it is liable to put the focus on liberating elements of the consumption experience, when close to the surface it continues to reinforce some of the less desirable dimensions of a consumer society. In other words, the more direct and the more experiential our engagement with sport, or the more we are able to convince ourselves that it is of our own making, the more it gets to control who and what we are.

As I indicated above, much of this appears, at least as far as those who actually partake in actual sporting activity, to be to do with sport as a form of embodied experience. For example, Hughson et al. (2005) reflect upon the relationship between the sportive body and both gender and class. In applying a phenomenological approach they thus debate the extent to which women experience forms of socialisation that construct them as body-subjects. The space women are able to 'feel' through their bodies is markedly more restricted than it is for men who have the benefit of a patriarchal society which encourages them to be 'sporting' in the way women are apparently not. The authors discuss sport as a form of cultural capital, and how participation in different sports reflects a person's class position and education, particularly as regards how this is reflected in the work of Pierre Bourdieu (1986). A good way of putting this is that the working classes are involved in what is effectively 'the taste of the necessary'. In other words, sport, like any other form of consumption activity, does not give consumers carte blanche to consume what they wish, but rather they are drawn to more of an instrumental as opposed to aesthetic approach to what it is they consume (Hughson et al., 2005).

Working-class consumers are thus deemed to be likely to be inclined towards instant forms of gratification as compared to the more reified tastes of the middle and upper classes. At a basic level this presents to us a vision of sports defined by class; notions of the upper classes engaging in hunting, fencing and polo; the middle class in yoga, running and rugby union; and the working classes in football, rugby league and boxing (often described by the media as a 'way out of the ghetto', wherever that might be). But the point is not only that your education and class determines your sporting interest, but that there are defining character-istics of these sports to which you are inevitably drawn. For example, the middle classes are allegedly drawn to sports that reward them in the longer term, while the working classes supposedly require the imme-diate gratification that the spectacle of the Premier League provides (Hughson et al., 2005). What the above discussion draws attention to is the way in which consumers 'feel' sport. We follow the sports we follow not out of free choice but as a product of the way our (class) history makes us see the world. Whether or not we can take Bourdieu's argu-ments at face value (there is an argument for saying, for example, that since he wrote his seminal work *Distinction*, class boundaries have been worn down and blurred), we can further reflect on how our individual experience of sport and the sporting spectacle may affect us differently depending on our background. You might argue then that the working classes, assuming they still exist in anything like the same form that they existed in the past, are more vulnerable to the kinds of compromising psycho-social processes I am discussing here. But ultimately what I am arguing is not that we are determined by the kinds of structures and influences that class implies, but rather that the experience society has gone as far as to, at least partially, transcend the class dynamic while simultaneously reinforcing it. It has so convinced us of our own ability to explore our unique paths of sporting passion that there exist in our own minds nothing but the world and the way we wish to inhabit that world. This might sound like a straightforward accusation of narcissism, but rather it constitutes a recognition that sports fans are being moulded in a very sophisticated fashion that maximises their commitment to consumption and undermines their ability to self-manage effectively. In this sense it isn't a form of selfishness, but a loss of self in a world of experience that promises precisely that.

We can celebrate sport for what it might do for the care of the self, but ultimately it will always operate as a site of pleasure and domination:

> It involves both the imposition of authority from above and the joy of autonomy from below. It exemplifies the exploitation of the labour process, even as it delivers autotelic pleasures ... The elevation of sport as a transcendent form of life, beyond the social or embodying its best aspects, is ridiculous. Conversely, the notion of sport as a technique of the self that is equally a technique of domination makes sense. (Miller, 2009: 190)

Of course, we still run our everyday existence through our commitments, relationships and aspirations, but we spend half of our time escaping these through the world of experience that consumption provides. But to describe this as an escape is simply not enough. You could argue, of course, that far from constituting any kind of demonstration of a higher and more sinister ideological plane, what it in fact delivers is some of the essential characteristics of the so-called leisure society that I described in Chapter 1. But in my view such an interpretation would be misleading and idealistic. The experience society is defined by a state of affairs in which the individual is so individualised and so oriented to and accommodated by the experiences that this implies that what emerges is the equivalent – ironically, and indeed unfashionably – of what used to be described as a mass society. The mass society we see in a world of experience is one in which the self is further away from our grasp than ever before. We are not consumer dupes or victims in the way that members of the Frankfurt School are alleged to have argued, because the experiences with which we engage allow us to realise ourselves through consumption (see Swingewood, 1977). But the potential of what is undoubtedly a sophisticated process is immense: it gives to and it simultaneously takes away from the self in a way that is beyond our personal control, precisely because it *feels* so utterly real and it feels like it is of our own making. It is precisely in this sense that the experience society gives with one experience and yet takes away with another.

8

The Coffee Shop Experience

In this chapter I want to focus on one specific example of experiential consumption as a means of further developing the concept of the experience society, and in order to think a little more closely about what the shift towards experiential consumption can tell us about the changing nature of consumption as an ideological force. For this purpose I want to concentrate on the coffee shop as a kind of archetypal urban space within which experiential consumption can be said to thrive. The rise of the coffee shop has been exponential. Since the 1970s the number of coffee shops in the UK has risen from 10,000 to 24,000. Meanwhile, baristas serve up around 2.4 billion cups a year, while contributing just under £10 billion a year to the UK economy. This is nothing short of a high street, or indeed cultural, revolution; it being estimated that the number of coffee shops will overtake the number of pubs in the UK by 2030. This trend tells its own story. It speaks to a cultural transition away from the consumption of alcohol. British consumers are drinking less (21 to 25 pubs are shutting down in the UK every week), and when they do what they drink appears to be changing (Poulter, 2018). For example, gin and craft beer have become increasingly popular, while the pub is simultaneously being reimagined as a family experience. The marked changes in how consumers socialise tells us not only about changes in taste, but also about how the ways in which consumers socialise and the potential role that consumption has in making us who we are is also changing. The point is that it isn't so much what consumers choose to drink that is important. It is the *how* of consumption that underpins what it means to live in an experience society.

Why the Coffee Shop?

The coffee shop has long been a centre of fascination for observers of consumer culture. One particularly significant paper in establishing the territory in this regard is that of Thompson and Arsel (2004), whose contribution I want to consider in some depth. Thompson and Arsel focus specifically on Starbucks as a kind of cultural icon of globalising corporate capitalism, and in recognising as much I will pay particular attention to the Starbucks experience throughout the remainder of this chapter. Their starting point is not that global capitalism is all-conquering and homogenising, but rather that consumers have at least some potential to creatively appropriate the meaning that such places afford them. Thompson and Arsel accept that spaces such as Starbucks are designed to provide themed servicescapes that shape consumer lifestyles by 'functioning as a cultural model that consumers act, think and feel through' (2004: 632), and thus argue that Starbucks constitutes a hegemonic landscape that links together symbolic and competitive relationships to a dominant experiential brand.

But the point here is that the experiential brand does not operate single-handedly, it operates in conjunction with the consumer. A café flâneur is a pleasure seeker who revels in the spectacle that the café provides: this isn't merely about sociability, but also the transient experience of the consuming moment and the glimpse into other people's lives that the café provides (Thompson and Arsel, 2004). Thompson and Arsel recognise that consumers distinguish between the inauthenticity of the homogenised Starbucks experience and the higher ideals and authenticity of local coffee shops. They also distinguish between café flâneurs who experience the coffee shop as a spectacle and oppositional localists who see potential in the coffee shop for the bonding together of particular societal values and political persuasions. The latter group thus fail to see that the very same characteristics of global homogenisations that they condemn in Starbucks are also played out, arguably in a more subtle fashion, in their local coffee shop, thereby undermining the grounds upon which such places are deemed to be 'authentic'. It might indeed be more profitable to think of the coffee shop, and Starbucks in particular, as a kind of 'coffee theme park': a public space in which the consumer can have his coffee and drink it, feeling both anonymous and part of something at one and the same time. This is something that Grinshpun (2014) addresses in her work on Starbucks in Japan, in which she argues that the company uses a particular visual lexicon. This involves replacing memory with imagination in order to encourage consumers to make connections with a cultural past to which they cannot relate. It constitutes a 'borrowed landscape' in which consumers are able to shape their own cultural connection to a space that transcends geographical and historical specificities. Much like a theme park, Starbucks thus wraps the space in a kind of cultural veneer that packages the coffee experience so that consuming a gingerbread latte, for example, convinces the consumer that they are experiencing a non-Japanese cultural experience:

> Having developed a model of a global chain, and reinvented an everyday commodity as a source of long term consumer appeal, Starbucks provides a lens for comprehending how the interplay between foreign and local moods forges a new vocabulary of cultural branding … The global and local emerge not as a dichotomy, but rather as dynamic imagineered constructs, relations between which switch in accordance with the context. (Grinshpun, 2014: 360)

Starbucks as an Experiential Icon

Starbucks is a global icon; an institutionalised symbol of the power of the coffee experience. The company, worth around £60 billion, serves over 100 million customers a week in over 30,000 cafes in 78 countries (Aldridge, 2019). Starbucks is a coffee monolith and perhaps an archetype of how the consumer experience can be maximised for economic benefit. Howard Schultz (1997), the ex-CEO of Starbucks (1986–2000 and 2008–2017), outlines his vision for the company in his book *Pour Your Heart Into It: How Starbucks Built a Company One Cup at a Time*. For Schultz the success of Starbucks was founded on a brand that 'was unique and mystical, yet purely American' (1997: 107) and which effectively reinvented the coffee experience. But more important than even this, and the reason Starbucks is so important for the purposes of this book is how Starbucks' ordinariness typifies the way in which the American consumer relates to the marketplace, and how he or she does so *through* experience (Simon, 2009).

The notion of experience is pivotal to everything that Starbucks offers. It could even be said to be Starbucks' most important product insofar as coffee is a mere means to the end, namely human connection (Thompson, 2016). For Schultz (1997), the benefits of Starbucks lie in its ability to offer the consumer a spark of romance that takes them away from the routine of everyday life. Coffee is an affordable luxury; a kind of personal reward for getting through the day. More than that, a Starbucks store offers a mini-haven: a breath of fresh air that also offers the possibility (albeit rarely realised) of some kind of casual social interaction with a fellow member or members of the human race. The key to success for Starbucks lies in Schultz's recognition that the place to go to drink your coffee is more than the coffee itself. What Starbucks came to offer was what Thompson (2016) describes as 'performed empathy', a place rooted in belonging, often in gentrifying parts of the city that could boast a particularly cool and noticeably bohemian urban vibe. It is in this context that Schultz reflects on Oldenburg's (1989) contention that coffee shops constitute a third place: a non-threatening space of informality outside of home and work. A third place fulfils the human need for communion; a neutral place that makes informed connections possible and perhaps most importantly a space that is available to all:

> Third spaces … serve to expand possibilities, whereas formal associations tend to narrow and restrict them. Third places counter the tendency to be restrictive in the enjoyment of others by being open to all and by laying emphasis on qualities not confined to status distinctions current in society. Within third places, the charm and flavor of one's personality, irrespective of his or her station in life, is what counts. (Oldenburg, 1989: 24)

From this point of view the third place that the coffee shop provides breaks down status distinctions, and allows the individual's personality to rise to the surface, providing the individual with what feels like a democratic experience. In short, the coffee shop has the potential of offering us a sense of community where community is otherwise declining. But is this something that the coffee shop can genuinely provide in a world which is so starkly individualised and thus further and further away from the kind of sentimental communitarianism that such a vision implies? After all, how often do strangers actively communicate in a coffee shop setting? Don't relatively anonymous chains such as Starbucks offer the reverse: aren't they public settings for private escapes? Most of all, do we even want our communities to be defined through the consumption of experience? This raises some important questions about sociality in the coffee shop and how this might be played out.

The Coffee Shop as Class/Status-driven Experience

Some authors have reflected on the role of the coffee shop as sites in which class is 'done' (Yodanis, 2006; Robinson, 2014). An argument can be made that such spaces facilitate a particular kind of aspiration and a commitment to progress. In the case of Robinson's work, the café environment allows young people in India to engage in forms of conspicuous consumption that distinguishes them from their role in the more traditional world advocated by their elders. The café effectively provides space in which this new generation can begin to feel at home in an emerging capitalist modernity. The café plays a prominent role in a process that suggests that free markets are an essential ingredient in the experience of a freer life: importantly a life not only to be imagined but one that can feasibly be *experienced*. As such the café took on a significance in India that amounted to more than the sum of its parts. It symbolised a way forward for social change and it made it real. And the emphasis here was on the expression of self; a considerable shift from traditional Indian notions of familial and caste interdependence (Robinson, 2014). For Robinson, café culture was suggestive of an untapped freedom. Whereas traditionally in India 'a person's agency and self-realization … were not conceptualized as independent from the will of others, tradition, religion and custom, but in accordance with them' (Robinson, 2014: 118), the café provided something else: a space that allowed them to hang out and to engage in new ways of thinking about, dreaming of and imagining an alternative way of life. The café may seem an insignificant space in isolation. But, as Robinson demonstrates, such spaces have the potential to be much more powerful than they might seem as a means of people 'making and remaking' themselves while challenging the relationship between the local and the global in the process.

The example above tells us something important about the aspirational nature of the coffee shop experience, something as important in a café in a high street in northern England as it is in Pune. There is no doubt, for example, that the type of coffee a person consumes can have a significant class dimension. However, this might be less about who sits where and interacts with whom in the coffee shop and more about who doesn't step through the doors in the first place. As Hartmann (2011) suggests, what is referred to as the third wave of coffee consumption is steeped in elitism and what might be referred to as coffee snobbism around the whys and wherefores of specialised coffee-making knowledge and artisanship. What's important is that the experience isn't freely available or automatic, but rather that it is the product of a set of circumstances created by Starbucks. As a company Starbucks initiates its customers into this third wave. It depends on its customers buying into thinking and experiencing coffee in this way. As Hartmann puts it, the company effectively creates a hermeneutic for its product so that experience is much more than about consuming better coffee, but rather about the social, cultural and economic conditions that underpin the coffee experience. Indeed, 'What we hear, and what we taste, when we encounter speciality coffee is not entirely attributable to the coffee – there is always someone behind the scenes, feeding our cup its lines' (2011: 179).

Making Customers Special

One key strand of contemporary social theory in recent decades, to which I shall return in the conclusion to this chapter, has been around the degree to which the contemporary social world is fragmented and how the uncertainties of that world have a knock-on effect for our sense of identity: space mediates our subjective bodies and the sense of self that we construct for our selves. Dickinson (2002) argues that Starbucks exploits this process: it offers a space in which the taste for coherency can be quenched. For example, Starbucks goes out of its way to accentuate its commitment to the natural world, not just through the coffee itself but via a broader orientation towards nature. What's interesting about this is that 'It is increasingly clear that our bodies do not, by themselves, found or justify our experience, nor can they support the weight of our claims to identity or selfhood. And so, we enter into the naturalism of Starbucks in hope of catching a glimpse of the possibility of the return of the body as a natural and foundational object' (Dickinson, 2002: 15). Simon (2009) describes the above as an effort on the part of Starbucks to achieve a careful balancing act between the consumer's quest for the predictable and the authentic. The whole ritual around coffee – the cultural capital consumers attach to it for example – further intensifies this process. You could go as far as to argue that Schultz went about romanticising coffee through aroma and the reiteration of value. He thus created a notion of coffee knowledge that the consumer could take home in order to feel good about their personal relationship to coffee (Ellis, 2004). The consumer thus revels in the self-flattery that they are capable of being a connoisseur of coffee (see also Ritzer, 1993).

We come to associate drinking coffee at a coffee shop as a personal treat or gift, but it's arguably only the 'leisured classes' that have access to such a clear-cut privilege. Their ability to buy a £3 cup of coffee at Starbucks is testament to their ability to belong (Dickinson, 2002). Starbucks becomes a haven, for those who can afford it, for treating the self well: the act of drinking the coffee frees us from the sins of the outside world. The consumption of coffee in Starbucks thus fulfils the role of a ritual and what Dickinson (2002) calls a 'stabilizing tradition' or indeed a sacred space. The following statement summarise this process to a tee:

> As we utilise Starbucks space of the (re)naturalized body, we have to recognize that we are grasping for coordinates in the very space that works to destroy the coordinates of the self. For the self is undone by urbanization and globalization; by access to excess, by the confrontation and covering of difference, and by the place destroying logic of consumer capitalism. Institutionally, Starbucks is this very sort of place. It serves up standardized coffee in standardized settings to standardized people. It expands aggressively across the globe. And, perhaps most damagingly, it proffers a globalized consumer practice as a response to the disorientation brought on by globalized consumer practices. In short, it provides globalized images and globalized spaces as resources for localizing bodies. (Dickinson, 2002: 22)

Venkatraman and Nelson (2008) acknowledge in their work on the consumption of Starbucks in China that the whole experience and indeed the ambience of Starbucks is closely managed, but that the end result is the availability of a public–private space in which a person's troubles can be forgotten and peace can be found. To put it another way, Starbucks provides a set of circumstances in which consumers can be themselves, a kind of 'backstage' where they can just *be*. Interestingly, what made the space particularly beneficial to Venkatraman and Nelson's Chinese respondents was the fact that in their eyes Starbucks offered an American experience (which is ironic given Starbucks' efforts are in fact all about creating a pseudo-Italian one). But more interesting is the fact that this research found that the actual drinking of coffee was fairly incidental to these customers' Starbucks experience. Rather, according to Venkatraman and Nelson, Starbucks provides a service-scape that actively supports consumers' processes of self-definition. From this point of view Starbucks is a meaningful partner in the process of identity creation: it is a meaningful place in which consumers can sit back and reflect on who it is they are outside of the actual circumstances that determine this. The suggestion here is that places such as Star-bucks come to the fore at a time, at least in China, when consumers are looking to live more of a life of their own rather than one determined for them by familial tradition (see Miles, 2007). In effect, the relatively friendly non-judgemental space that Starbucks provides is deemed to be a positive space, and a personal metaphor for the individual's ability to self-manage.

The above point is worth reflecting upon in some depth because it pro-vides us with a slightly different slant on the debate regarding what we mean by a meaningful experience in the first place. It is not just that places like Starbucks offer an experience per se, it is the way in which such expe-rience is used in the process of self-construction that matters. To this end Venkatraman and Nelson quote Manzo (2003), who argues that places become meaningful as symbols of key life events, and that in moments of personal reflection this is what gives them their meaning. For Manzo this means that our environments become increasingly important to us at times of disruption, say after a burglary or a natural disaster, when home in particular comes into the forefront of our consciousness. Thus, 'People choose environments that are congruent with their self-concept, modi-fying settings to better represent themselves, or moving to find places which are more congruent with their sense of self' (Manzo, 2003: 54). The focus in Manzo's work tends to be on ruptures in our experience of place which reinforce their significance. What if the ideological impact of con-sumption is such that it has come to affect our lives more profoundly than such an approach would suggest? What if the potential of our mundane everyday experiences to contribute to a sense of self have been magnified by the experiences that consumption provides?

Behind the Façade

In discussing what constitutes a third place, Oldenburg contends that the environment in which modern life is lived in is in fact a dictatorial force that adds or takes away experiences as and when it sees fit. In a sense the coffee shop is a psycho-social space: it provides something of an escape. It deliberately offers a range of personal benefits to the individual; a means of delighting and sustaining him or her through the mutual stimulation that the assemblage of people it provides implies: 'The third place is largely a world of its own making, fashioned by talk and quite independent of the institutional order of the larger society. If the world of the third place is far less consequential than the larger one, its regulars find abundant compensation in the fact that it is a more decent one, more in love with people for their own sake, and, hour for hour, a great deal more fun' (Oldenburg, 1989: 48). Perhaps Oldenburg's (1989) somewhat sentimental view of the third place reflects a world in which consumers are easily diverted; a world of experience that deflects us from a deeper underlying reality. Oldenburg believes that the third place offers a spiritual tonic, a freedom from social obligations and an 'optimal staging of self'; but perhaps the point is that such spaces provide nothing more than a cocoon, a breathing space that is less about a release from the traumas of the everyday and more about their maintenance through the pretence that they are escapable in the first place. Indeed, as Thompson (2016) notes, what Starbucks denotes more than anything is the privatisation of social experience, to the extent that Starbucks isn't in fact selling a product at all, 'but a set of social relations – a way of inhabiting your city and your world' (2016: 205).

It's no coincidence that Randall (2015) uses the coffee shop as his point of departure in discussing the ways in which everyday life is enmeshed in storytelling. He describes the coffee shop as a sacred place, a sanctuary in which he is able to be himself, a place in which his 'internal space' opens up before him through the lens that everyday humanity provides. But as Randall points out, the sense of escapist fulfilment experienced in the coffee shop is not achieved in isolation from the broader society in which we live. This is a thought that the cultural commentator Peter York (2014) also reflects upon in his book, *Authenticity is a Con*, when he discusses the rise of the so-called 'me' generation and the difficulties inherent in realising one's full potential and connecting to one's true self in the process. Authenticity from this point of view is to be found in a person's feelings, assertions and judgements, in the way in which they find a route through the impossible standards of expectation that determine them and which leave us all in a constant state of divorce from our authentic self. What can be identified in the above analysis is a recognition that how consumers experience Starbucks, and coffee shops more generally, has significant personal implications:

> While seeking an experience of public life and participation in a broader social spectacle, café flâneurs' third-place consumption practices are motivated by an apolitical quest for enjoyable and edifying forms of identity-play, and they express little desire for communal relationships steeped in shared political and civic aims (and their concomitant nexus of reciprocal obligations). (Thompson and Arsel, 2004: 640)

This question of identity and how it can be played out through the experience of place is addressed more directly in the work of Dickinson (2002), who considers the significance of everyday spaces and how they are visited and reconstructed in non-conscious ways. What's significant about this is that it is through the 'interstices of the everyday' that we effectively materialise ourselves and our bodies. The mundane provides the platform upon which we construct subjectivities: Starbucks effectively provides an arena within which this process is graphically manifested and, more importantly, through which it is *felt*. From this point of view, what Starbucks does is provide a space in which a coherent or stable sense of self can be realised on what are in fact very unstable foundations.

Managing the Coffee Shop Experience

What we do know is that the coffee shop experience is highly managed. More than that, Starbucks in particular can be understood to portray the virtues of an experience-focused design which constructs how the consumer feels. This is a form of design that self-consciously engages with all the senses in order to maximise, albeit subconsciously, the impact of the experience on the consumer (Clark, 2008). The success of such design is undoubtedly founded upon the notion of familiarity. Consumers are attracted to what they have come to see as feeling comfortable over time. It is not an exaggeration to say that Starbucks, as an urban icon, comes to contribute to how we define ourselves and the world in which we live (Fellner, 2008). Starbucks doesn't simply reflect the broader culture in which it sits; it actively reinforces that culture: 'The café counterculture has been, by definition, a bastion of intellectual and class privilege, created to distinguish the superior cool and élan of its habitués' (Fellner, 2008: 138).

As far as Starbucks is concerned, what has gone on over time is a reinvention. Starbucks 'polished up' its image as a place for artisanal relaxation and 'invited in the masses' (Fellner, 2008: 138). Reinvented as an ethical organisation, Starbucks was able to position itself as mainstream and yet (mildly) alternative (Heath and Potter, 2005). Fellner (2008) puts her finger on the appeal of Starbucks when she talks about the choice of coffee shops that consumers have at their disposal. There may be a whole variety of cool options to choose between, but if in doubt go to Starbucks. It may not change your life, but at least you know you can find yourself there because with Starbucks you know what you are going to get. Starbucks offers the consumer a small yet meaningful and affordable luxury, but it does so while concealing the reality that lies behind the myth (a longing for global dominance, anti-union practices and cultural conformity) and by encouraging a soporific complacency. Starbucks encourages its customers to linger, but it does so in the context of a highly controlled, surveilled and regulated environment (Ellis, 2004). Equally important in this regard is the changing composition of the coffee house and the fact it has had to adapt over time. For Ellis (2004) the coffee shop operates as a barometer of social change, and he talks about the role that the coffee house and more specifically the espresso bar played long ago as an associative space that was both subversive and exotic. This was an entrepreneurial space in which notions of civic authority were challenged. But the difference between the espresso bar and the Starbucks of today is that the latter is less associative and more self-contemplative. Starbucks succeeded because it offered the consumer a higher-quality product based on significantly improved and more relaxing spaces which were located where the customer most needed them. What we can identify here is a shift from the coffee shop as a place for teenage rebellion and cultural transgression, to that of a chain that symbolises the tranquil docility of consumerism as a way of life.

Working Coffee

It is of course also important to remember that it is not only the consumer whose identity is affected by the coffee shop experience. In her discussion of affective labour in Melbourne's café culture, Cameron (2018) discusses the so-called democratisation of self that occurs in a neoliberal context and how the individual is routinely expected to redefine the structural constraints that they are confronted with. What's described here is a 'symbolically charged' metropolitan city in which a particularly affective type of labour makes the worker obliged to do his or her part in ensuring that the company brand is made to be 'emotionally contagious' and communicate an appropriately 'hip' vibe. This adds up to what is essentially a performance: a commodification of communication and a camouflaging of production in which human emotional qualities become a key part of the culture of the service being provided. And what's important here is that the demands of the consumer are simultaneously established and met *through* the performance (see also Lazzarato, 2006):

> Not only are customers moved by the experience, but more pressingly, workers and employers, too, are seduced by atmosphere and vulnerable to the impact of 'the moment' to the point where, in fact, nobody is actually in control. Being pleasurably moved in the short term, at work, simultaneously blocked workers from achieving their goals and from seeing a long term trajectory, while, at the same time, powerfully seducing them with autonom, creative expression, flexible hours, spontaneous joy, transparency and authenticity in their interactions, thinking in the moment and being present. If they were moved with joy, they would very likely provide better service and personally invest in the venue and their employer. Stimulated by pleasure, they were empowered to (lucratively) embody the venue's image. Feelings and ecologies of interaction between workers, the spaces, customers, employers, and the brand more generally – the sensory conditions that they encounter and feel – help to determine the overall value generated by these venues well beyond simple monetary terms. (Cameron, 2018: 14–15)

I talked in more depth about the changing experience of the sensory workplace in Chapter 4. At this stage it's more important to consider the suggestion that the this isn't a one-way process. Rather, the consumer and those employed to provide the consumer experience self-consciously wrap themselves in the experiences that society provides. Let me offer one example. I am a great film lover. It's not necessarily the films them-selves that I love but the experience I associate with those films. For me, Saturday nights are film night. They are precious to me: a focal point in my week in which I settle down with a glass or two of red wine, the cat on my lap and a good film. This is 'me time'. I look forward to not nec-essarily the relaxation that these moments bring, but rather the thought that they will. I spend a lot of time thinking about what films I might watch, often choosing them the night before, in order to maximise and prolong the pleasure. I am constructing an experience around the film and I am at the very centre of that experience. In effect, I become the experience. The film is merely the vehicle in which I at least am able to become the most me I can be.

Conclusion

The coffee shop is an ideological space. Its ideological power lies in its ability to offer the possibility of self-work. It's in this context that Cameron (2018) reflects upon the so-called post-modern era as a time in which human beings are in a constant hunt of affirmation, and what Lasch (1979) describes as an 'absurdist theatre of the self' in which labour power as well as consumer power are defined through the cult of personality. Cameron goes on to discuss the work of Richard Sennett (1998), who points out that the individual's thirst for experience is built upon a psyche characterised by a collage of identities. The individual thus 'dwells in a state of endless becoming – a selfhood which is never finished' (1998: 133). Similarly, Lifton (1995) describes the existence, or at least the potential emergence, of the protean self; a fluid kind of selfhood appropriate to the restless uncertainty of our age. The protean self is defined by its ability to maintain its poise or balance and is defined by the ability to feel and experience a common humanity. Lifton (1995) thus aspires to a more hopeful world in which the dual goals of authen-ticity and belonging become realistic, and in which how we choose to experience the world becomes more strategic.

Of course, the debate around the fragmented nature of identity in a so-called post-modern world, and the suggestion that we effectively pick and choose our identities and adapt from one set of circumstances to another, have long been disputed and could indeed be argued to be little more than a product of theoretical fashion and whimsy. The post-structuralist notion that the self effectively ceases to exist in a world beyond that of the fragmented decentred subject is something I shall return to in Chapter 9. At this stage it is worth pointing out that such debates have tended to look at the way in which difference is 'internal' as well as external, so that any notion of the self is a product of difference within our selves as well as in a comparison between ourselves and others. There is something important to be said here, particularly regarding Sennett's (1998) notion that the contemporary self is pliant and always open to the possibilities of new experience as part of its constant craving for coherence in a world that promotes multiple rather than single narratives. In a sense this is all about the democratisation of self-expression and the onus on the individual to redefine the structural constraints they face on a personal basis (Cameron, 2018).

The above process isn't a natural or 'authentic' one: it is one that is both constructed and reproduced economically. In this sense, coffee shops are the product of a 'mood economy' in which the coffee shop employee him or herself feels everything and is committed to inducing customers into *feeling* and experiencing the atmosphere as fully as possible. This is all part of the reframing of late capitalist ideology as common sense, and a commitment to the idea that structural limitations are ultimately secondary to the power of the individual to overcome the circumstances in which their selfhood is implied. In short, the individual tempers the volatility of labour market conditions through a protracted search for a sense of spontaneity and momentary belonging. In effect, the worker becomes cocooned in a cyclical 'mood ring' (Massumi, 2015) of intensity in which the intensity of the experience becomes everything (Cameron, 2018).

Another useful way of understanding the changing nature of the self and its relationship to social change in the context of coffee as experience is perhaps through Melucci's (1996) phenomenological notion of play in which he conceives of the self as a set of highly subjective and intimate experiences which are constructed in relation to social structural dynamics. The accelerated pace of change, the multiplicity of roles assumed by the individual, the deluge of messages that wash over us expand our cognitive and affective experience to an extent that is unprecedented in human history: 'The search for a safe haven for the self becomes an increasingly critical understanding, and the individual must build and continuously rebuild her/his "home" in the face of the surging flux of events and relations' (Melucci, 1996: 2). A key element of the self's relationship to social change is, for Melucci, the paradox of choice: the more choice we have the more difficult it becomes to manage our experience. The complexity of the social world immeasurably extends the range of experiences available to us, but our ability to utilise such experiences, to make them real, is inevitably constrained, and uncertainty is the result. In other words, the availability of life choices entails an *obligation* to choose (Melucci, 1996). Such a state of affairs creates a feeling that we must perpetually seek out new experiences for their own sake:

> We cannot escape our symbolic inclusion in a cosmopolitan culture which expands and multiplies the possible worlds of our experience, while at the same time confronting us with their complexity and the necessity to make choices. Complexity signifies differentiation, high speed and frequency of change, and broadening of opportunities for action. (Melucci, 1996: 44)

Melucci's argument is particularly telling when he reflects on what this all means for the stability of the self. In his view human beings are constantly looking out for change, which is a double-edged sword insofar as it offers the promise of fulfilling our desires while being shadowed by a fearfulness and anxiety that we can never quite shake off. Let me offer a further trivial and yet meaningful example of what Melucci describes. I have dinner envy. If I ever go to a restaurant for dinner, I will spend a long time contemplating the choices available to me convinced that it is impossible to find the one single choice that is right for me. I will eventually plump for my selection. Almost certainly it seems that my dining companion will choose something that I might well have chosen myself, and when it arrives I discover that, sure enough, it was a preferable choice to my own. Herein lies the everyday dangers of experience. Through experience we find ourselves and yet we lose ourselves as a result. Melucci says that this sense of loss is inevitable. Every choice is partial and as such unfulfilling, and yet the society in which we live convinces us that we can find ourselves *through* experience. And we are permanently exhausted by this. The more experiences we seek the less we are ourselves.

The coffee shop provides a useful lens through which we can begin to learn more about the psycho-social consequences of the experience society. Of course, coffee shops are the product of a long history and of having been located in particular societal contexts. They are geographically specific and, for good or bad, such specificity can be adapted (e.g. in the example of Schultz's (1997) admiration of the Italian coffee house and his determination to reproduce this in an American guise). But what's most intriguing about the coffee shop, and in particular the coffee shop chain, is its sheer ubiquity. At this moment in time the city of Manchester where the author currently resides has 49 Costas, 17 Starbucks, 17 Caffè Nerros, four Coffee Republics, three Ritazzas and two Pumpkins. On the one hand this might tell us something about the familiar and routinised ways in which consumers like to spend their time and money. But from another perspective it might well tell us something more profound about how it is we are changing as consumers. When Schulze (1995) first talked about the emergence of an experience society he reflected upon a world in which life had effectively become an 'experience project': that our challenge lay in best designing our own lives, the problems of the everyday being situational and more subjective in nature. One interpretation of Schulze's work might be that the emergence of the experience society is democratic insofar as the pleasures of experience have come to be situated at the foreground of selfhood; but democracy is rarely what it seems.

Depending on who you listen to, coffee is going through its third (with an emphasis on high-quality artisanal) or fourth (organically produced and fair traded) wave. Such transitions in part owe a debt to Starbucks, which foretold the story around the added experiential value that high-quality coffee could provide while also using the ethical dimension of coffee production as a selling point (Hartmann, 2011). Interestingly, Hartmann (2011) describes this as being part of a neoliberal fantasy capable of convincing the consumer that they are not only buying a unique coffee experience, but that they can pat themselves on the back for doing so in an ethical fashion. Of course, it's not the sense of doing what's right that does the trick here, but rather the cultural capital that the consumer can procure as a result. This is a peculiarly self-indulgent process:

Self-giving is a way of signalling one's worth in a world that seems to revolve around market fundamentalism and the profit motive. Your purchase of a fancy drink is an investment in oneself, an affirmation of self-worth in an age of relentless consumerism. Solace takes on a dollar value. The market provides a tangible, affordable cup of affirmation. It is in this sense that self-gifting is fully rational – it observes the basic postulates of the free market in its practice. (Hartmann, 2011: 169)

For Simon (2009), self-gifting is a kind of self-choreographed retail therapy. Consumption gives us comfort and solace in a world that otherwise rarely appears to do so. A visit to Starbucks is calculated in the sense that it has a value beyond the physical consumption of the coffee itself. The Starbucks experience allows the consumer to convince themselves that they are in control: that they are taking hold of the moment for their own experiential ends. Starbucks tapped into this process by presenting their cafes to the consumer as 'three-dimensional environments for self-gifting' (Simon 2009: 134).

What we can identify here is a process during which the focus of Starbucks shifted from an aesthetic of authenticity that could no longer be sustained as it reached critical mass, towards one of commercial necessity, including the selling of non-coffee beverages and merchandise such as books and music (Hartmann, 2011). The irony is that by going down this route the coffee experience became less 'authentic' than ever: the more personally authentic forms of consumption feel to the individual, the less authentic they actually are. This is a hallmark of the experience society and one that was reflected in the global store design strategy Starbucks launched in 2009. By 2009 the brand identity of Starbucks and the quality of its product had arguably been diluted by mass customisation (Aiello and Dickinson, 2014). In response to this the design strategy for new stores began to focus on actively hiding the Starbucksness of Starbucks in favour of the symbolic experience of a local ambience. Indeed, the success of Starbucks was built in part upon its ability to claim the space that civic institutions had occupied in the past, while doing so in such a way that it was able to delve deeply into customers' personal and socially situated consciousness. This reflects a broader process in which everyday 'associationalism' has declined in the United States, creating a situation in which the middle classes in particular are apparently increasingly detached from one another and in which any notion of the public (in the form of shopping malls for instance), for good or bad, became increasingly disparate (Simon, 2009). This drift from the public to the private opened up a space into which companies like Starbucks could ameliorate the tensions that existed around our desire to belong and yet retain our sense of individuality at one and the same time.

Starbucks deliberately reasserted its relationship to the community and attempted to bring that community into its space. What is more, there was an onus on customers' active experience of such spaces through the less formulaic visuals and the tactile surfaces that the new strategy promoted. So Starbucks, a company founded on the determination to reconstruct the fairly mundane act of drinking a coffee as an experience, was demonstrably taking that experience to the next level by liberating the degree of consumer choice in how consumers might go about experiencing such spaces. This represents a slowing up of the Starbucks experience; the customer is encouraged to linger in the community that the space implies (Aiello and Dickinson, 2014). But most important of all, such creativity comes at a cost. It is manifested through a very particular racialised and class-based vision of what community actually means. This is a strategy that feeds off the cultural capital of its envisaged clientele and reinforces such capital in such a way that the ideological processes it is engaged with are reinforced and intensified. Starbucks' design strategy is far from neutral in its intent. It is designed to create a controlled environment in which creativity is only achieved at the behest of a company resituating itself in relation to the rapidly emerging independent coffee sector. As Aiello and Dickinson (2014: 318) put it, 'As a form of emplaced and embodied cosmopolitanism, Starbucks' strategy of locality may contribute to further solidifying a capitalism that makes us, quite aptly, feel close and even become part of its matter.'

The point I want to conclude with in this chapter, and one that I want to consider in more detail in Chapter 9, is that although we appear to live in increasingly knowing times – in times of cynicism and of fakery – such sentiments are more symptomatic of the omnipresence of the experience society than of its dilution. In other words, such cynicism props up the experience society rather than weakens it. It is not that consumers are simply apathetic and that coffee shops are spaces where apathy rules, but rather that consumers are increasingly fascinated by the temporally finite nature of the experiences available to them. Coffee shops can have considerable potential as regards the transformation of bodily practices that relate consumers to key aspects of social change, for example (Robinson, 2014). Above all, the coffee shop provides an arena in which anything *feels* possible. My contention here is that the appeal of chains of coffee shops such as Starbucks lies in the momentary sense of respite and one-ness, less in the experience of the coffee than the space for selfhood that the coffee excuses. In this sense the experience society could actually be said to provide a hiatus from the kind of boredom that characterises what is more broadly a homogenised consumer landscape. People engage more closely in the experience of consumption as a means of reflecting on their own selfhood, not in a cynical way, but because such reflection frees them from cynicism and provides what at that moment feels like a pure space in which only the self matters. The problem with this, of course, is that such spaces are not unadulterated, they are ideological spaces: spaces that have been constructed to provide just that experience (see Schultz, 1997). As Craib (1998: 176) puts it, 'Neither the self nor identity are simple social products, rather in the end they are areas of individual and collective freedom which are constantly threatened by the structure and the ideologies of the wider society.' From the experience society there is no escape. The consumer is complicit in his or her own 'ensnarement' in the experiences that the experience society can offer (see Simon, 2009). The Starbucks experience is a meaningful one for the consumer; but perhaps it is meaningful because of what it tells us about how we are manipulated as consumers, rather than about the ability of the individual to be in control.

9

Consumer Capitalism Rebooted

The world of consumption has been radically transformed in the past 20 to 30 years. Consumer capitalism has rebooted. Since the heady days of the late twentieth century, in which the consumer society seemed to make anything seem possible, we have gradually come to a different place where what we consume appears to be more a matter of social and personal retrospection. We appear, albeit painfully slowly, to be recognising the impact of consumption on the environment, and today there is perhaps more of a stigma attached to unfettered forms of consumption than ever before. The regularity of television programmes about how we might consume less, and countless online articles focusing on elements of mindfulness and self-discipline, might be said to be demonstrative of a change of heart. Consumption has changed, but there may be more to the nature of this trajectory than we might assume. The experience society is clearly about much more than a transition from the consumption of products to the consumption of experiences. And although we can acknowledge that patterns of consumption are, broadly speaking, moving in just such a direction, what's more important here is the contention that the way we experience the process of consumption is itself undergoing something of a reinvention. The experience society is therefore not simply a society defined by the ability of consumers to purchase pre-packaged experiences, but by an evolved notion of the ideological connotations of the consumption experience: consumption is arguably changing how we relate to our *selves*. Most worryingly perhaps, the rebooting of consumer capitalism through the personalisation of culture as experience has created a new orthodoxy in which, regardless of societal pressures to be otherwise, a self fulfilled through consumption is ultimately and personally nothing to be ashamed of. In these circumstances the consumer becomes more pliable. It's in this sense that the experience society constitutes, above all, a state of mind, in which any notion of an all-powerful consumer capitalism obliging people to consume in particular ways is deemed inconsequential, acceptable even, given that the mere act of just allowing this to happen, the sense that we matter after all, is liberating enough in itself.

We only have to look around us to recognise how commodified experiences are becoming ever more pertinent to how we experience the social world, and indeed elements of social change. Butsch (1990) argues that, in the United States at least, we can identify a shift from time-intensive to goods-intensive recreation that occurred around the turn into the twentieth century. The family-oriented consumer culture that came to fruition in the 1950s was later supplanted by a much more individualised version of consumption in which the transformation of selfhood came to the fore (Hurley, 2001). At this time the urban landscape became a physical representation of class-based aspiration. But as class itself became less and less important (or at least appeared to be so), and the transformation of self came to be so tied up in how we consumed, consumer capitalism sought to find new and subtle ways of imposing such a regime. Broadly, this entailed the increasing role of the symbolic and how consumers came to embrace design, style, luxury and the like, as a means of endowing consumer goods with additional self-related meanings. The thesis underpinning this book is that this process has effectively exhausted itself. In an environment in which the environmental wisdom of consumption is increasingly problematised, and in which human beings have broadly questioned their relationship to products, experiences have stepped into the impasse. This is not something that has happened overnight, but is part of a recalibration or reboot of consumer capitalism that is connected to broader parallel processes of regeneration, gentrification and identity politics. Hence the emergence of spaces of experiential consumption: of ethnic markets, themed restaurants, tattoo parlours, café culture and gentrified market food halls, all of which hint at not only a long-term shift away from the mass market and towards the freedom of individual agency, but also at a more subtle explosion of choice in the where and how as opposed to the what people consume.

Conceptualising Experience

In order to get to the crux of what I mean, and how this represents some kind of a transition in how consumer capitalism conducts the essence of selfhood in its own guise, I want to briefly reflect upon some of the major contributors that have shone light on the changing nature of experience over the last century, while more importantly reflecting on what the combined insights of these approaches can tell us about what it means to be a consumer in an experience society. The first point to make in this regard is that as a theorist, or at least as someone seeking to understand some of the complexities of the human condition, I am wholeheartedly married to the notion that the consumer is no more completely controlled in a consumer or an experience society than he or she has free rein to be what he or she wishes. In other words, consumption is as much a sociological as it is as psychological process, and may be best described, albeit perhaps unfashionably, as *psycho-social*.

Consumer capitalism works, or at least purports to work, insofar as we buy into the world it creates. Experience is a key part of that. Perhaps one of the most significant contributions around the role of experience in selfhood is that of Dewey (2005) who is interested specifically in the aesthetic experience of art. What's important about Dewey's contribution is his contention that the relationship between the consumer of art and the art itself is mutually determinative. An individual does not simply consume a piece of art, the art is simultaneously a participant in a process of self-construction. From this point of view, Dewey's concept of the self, as Benson (1993) points out, is not an isolated entity, detached from social life, but an active and interactional one. Far from being fixed, the self is responsive to the context in which it finds itself and depends upon the experiences in which it is implicated. This creates a context in which there are rich pickings for the capitalist machine that gleefully exploits the self in order to maximise its potential as a cog in its own plan for indomitable reproduction.

These reflections serve to demonstrate the extent to which debates over the nature of experience is a philosophical minefield (see Lash, 2018 for one such example). It has not been the purpose of this book to grapple with the philosophical subtleties of such debates. However, I do want to emphasise the notion that experience is not a passive process and in fact tells us something profound about the nature of selfhood and its relationship to consumption at a time of rapid economic, social and political change. For this reason the work of Walter Benjamin (2005a, 2005b) is particularly instructive. Benjamin helps us reflect upon how social change, at least in part, determines the nature of experience. He

laments what he considered to be the methodical destruction of experience. His argument is that social change at the beginning of the twentieth
century was unmanageably rapid, while 'in a field of force of destructive
torrents and explosions, was the tiny fragile human body' (Benjamin,
2005b: 732). This was an agenda for change that was at the behest of
the ruling powers and which was defined above all by the unavoidable
terrors of poverty. Experience was, according to Benjamin, withered by
the force of such changes, people's existence was not only determined
by the needs of commerce, but it had become virtually non-existent so
that human beings' control over it was virtually nil. In effect, experience
becomes deeply superficial: an individual is little more than a product of
experiences passed on to him or her through commodification,

> because he never raises his eyes to the great and the meaningful, the
> philistine has taken experience as his gospel. It has become for him a
> message about life's commonness. But he has never grasped that there
> exists something other than experience, that there are values-inex-
> perienceable – which we serve ... Why is life without meaning or
> solace for the philistine? Because he knows experience and nothing
> else. Because he himself is desolate and without spirit. And because
> he has no inner relationship to anything other than the common and
> the always-already-out-of-date. (Benjamin, 2005a: 4)

What is being described here, although its author would not have
perhaps put it this way, is a loss of agency that is ideologically driven,
that is above and beyond the locus of control that any one individual can
depend upon. We can obviously object to some of the language being
used here, but the more important point to consider is that this kind
of process is in constant motion so that any kind of experience under
the remit of consumer capitalism is likely to be diluted by the process
of commodification in some shape or form. And of course, the more
diluted it becomes, the less the consumer is able to consume it without it
being 'contaminated' by commodification. It is safe to assume that when
Csikzentmihalyi (2002) talks about experience that is in itself rewarding – as a kind of flow that the person experiencing it wants to repeat as
often as possible – he did not have the consumer experience in mind.
Indeed, you could argue that consumption is the polar opposite to flow.
It is stilted, momentary, inevitably disappointing and unsustainable.

The experience society exploits this tension: experience is the vehicle through which the self can seek out a sense of fulfilment; it cannot be long-lasting, but it can at least *feel* meaningful.

As far as humanity is concerned, the world described by Benjamin is a catastrophic one. The whirlwind of progress in which we are all constantly implicated and apparently alienated is entirely deceptive. Indeed, the whole of human experience comes to be defined by the deceiving and fetishised power of the commodity form (see Hetherington, 2007). However, Benjamin, as Hetherington suggests, is not entirely pessimistic as far as he identifies a utopian bent in the human quest for experiences through luxury, comfort, abundance and the like. In this sense we are in the process of seeking out a place of happiness even if we cannot ultimately achieve it. The notion of a dreamlike existence is crucial here, as it hints at the power of experience, and how we reinvent that experience to live a good life. In other words, the key question is whether we can be anything other than alienated through our experiences, experiences that are inevitably the product of commodity fetishism? Does experience do anything more than detach the individual from social reality and the inequalities that underpin it? We have already established that there is an argument for saying that commodification represents the overriding state or condition of our time. Such a position would imply some kind of loss of 'authenticity', and a sense that the experience can never be fully possessed by its owner (Jay, 2005). Furthermore, our determination to make experiences our own, to individualise them in the present, cuts off the possibility of their value to use in our future connection with others. In this sense the experience society is a momentary one and this constructs the grounds upon which consumer capitalism continues to thrive.

In Chapter 2 I talked about the way in which the economics of consumption are increasingly dependent upon the service that surrounds a product rather than the product itself, and how consumption has become more about buying into the possibilities through which you can explore your self, so that the process of consumption and identification through consumption that the person goes through is more and more stylised and branded. This speaks to my broader concern that the psycho-social nature of our engagement with consumption, not least through the experience society, remains underexplored. What I am describing here amounts to more than the narcissist pursuit of pleasure or enjoyment, but it does reflect a state of affairs in which 'enjoyment is always conditioned by the practical and symbolic limitations of a society governed today in the interests of capital' (Cremin, 2011: 114). As I acknowledged above, the psychological and the social are inseparable (Stenner, 2017). The point is that consumer capitalism's emphasis on this relationship is such that the experience of self is confined to the very parameters that it sets. By filtering selfhood through intensified commodified experiences in which our sense of self is heightened, our sense of being that self is tied to a particular version of ourselves over which we have very limited control. The consumer cannot challenge him or self if, however momentarily exiting it might feel, that self is constrained by a narcissistic conception of what selfhood should be. The kind of belonging that the experience society promotes therefore barely constitutes any kind of belonging at all, but rather a kind of nothingness, an intensification of a one-dimensional self that amounts to an automatic response to the demands of the homogenised world that surrounds it (see Cremin, 2011). Experience is the fuel that makes all this possible.

What we are talking about here, in old-fashioned terms, is some kind of a transformation in the nature of the relationship between structure and agency. Some authors have developed the notion of 'social practices' (see Williams, 1980; Giddens, 1983; Butsch, 1990) as a way of understanding how people go about recreating structure through their everyday practice. The implication is that social life is more fluid than a straight structure and agency dualism will account for. In discussing Gramsci's (2005) notion of hegemony, Butsch (1990) argues that hegemony is embedded in consumer fun and that consumers are effectively complicit in shaping new products and services (and thus practices) which are shaped into various forms of capitalist profit. Of course, the fact that we might accept, in whatever shape or form, that human beings are engaged in some kind of proactive relationship with their consumption experience does not mean we should pay any less attention to the power dynamics that are being played out. For this reason it's interesting to reflect upon Butsch's discussion of hegemony, a focus that he claims 'encourages us to look for the forces and limits of control in the fabric of practices that constitute people's lived experience' (1990: 8). Butsch encourages us to consider the ways in which people's (in this case leisure) choices and activities are constrained, and that lived experience is simultaneously the primary arena within which capitalism ensures its durability. From this point of view power relations are embedded in the marriage between corporate profit and 'fun'. Capitalism thus thrives on its own ability to 'recreate' (in terms of pastimes and experiences) consumers, while simultaneously recreating their selves.

Mindful Capitalism

What is interesting about the above process is how much more sophisticated it is now than in the past. Such sophistication lies in the ability of capitalism to provide the consumer with the foundations upon which they can be more convinced than ever that they are free to assert their own selfhood in whichever way they see fit, while perpetuating the belief that they can do so without the interference of commodification, while all the while such interference is intensified. As a means of demonstrating my argument I want to consider an example of a modern-day phenomenon which graphically demonstrates the playing out of this kind of process: the fashion, fad or movement known as mindfulness. Mindfulness is all about the psychological deployment and experience of meditation and self-awareness in order to live in the present moment, while maximising one's own feelings, thoughts and bodily sensations. On the other hand, we could equally describe it as a lifestyle choice or a way of being that facilitates a particular kind of existence in a consumer society. On the surface mindfulness is about the individual taking control in such a way that the everyday is intensified, while the stress and anxiety of experience is dissipated through the power of self and self-awareness. But there is more going on here than meets the eye. Purser's (2019) critique of what he calls McMindfulness is particularly pertinent in this regard. He argues that far from the transformative effect on selfhood that mindfulness appears to imply, it can be better understood as a new kind of banal capitalist spirituality that simply serves to reinforce the neoliberal status quo. It is worth considering the above argument in more detail insofar as it speaks to the broader processes of experiential selfhood with which this book is concerned. Purser's point here is that mindfulness works on the principle that the causes of suffering exist within *our selves* and not within the broader social, economic and cultural contexts in which we live. By doing so mindfulness reinforces the destructive logic of contemporary capitalism. It encourages a state of affairs where the everyday management of stress becomes a *personal* enterprise. Any blame for the destructiveness of contemporary society is erased and the individual thus becomes responsible for his or her own positionality:

> The so-called mindfulness revolution meekly accepts the dictates of the market-place. Guided by a therapeutic ethos aimed at enhancing the mental and emotional resilience of individuals, it endorses neo-liberal assumptions that everyone is free to choose their responses, manage negative emotions and 'flourish' through various modes of self-care ... Void of a moral compass or ethical commitments, unmoored from a vision of the social good, the commodification of mindfulness keeps it anchored in the ethos of the market. (Purser, 201: 11–17)

What's particularly interesting about Purser's analysis is the proposition that through such processes neoliberal institutions actively reformulate what it means to be a human being and in doing so perpetuate what is a essentially an entrepreneurial notion of selfhood and self-management. This can be referred to as what both Purser (2019) and Giroux (2014) describe as a 'disimagination machine' adept at circulating images and representations which undermine the capacity of individuals to bear witness to a different and critical sense of remembering, agency, ethics and collective resistance and which are thus designed to preserve the status quo. The experience society manages to achieve a state of affairs in which agency feels ever more real in its promise, resulting in what Purser describes as an 'illusory separateness of self' (2019: 262). This is something that is closely related to Han's (2017) notion of psycho-politics, in which he considers the use of the psyche as a productive force capable of therapeutically optimising the individual. Spiritual practices are in this way co-opted for the purposes of social, economic and political control (Purser, 2019).

For Han (2017), this state of affairs reflects a point in history in which we are constantly refashioning and reinventing ourselves so that even class struggle has morphed into a struggle for and yet against the self. Capitalism frees us but in doing so 'individuals degrade into the genital organs of Capital' (2017: 4). Our need for experience is thus nothing more than an additional layer of delusion. From this perspective consumers are less defined by what it is they consume and more by the emotions they attach to how they consume, so that everyone exists in their own panoptican of consumption through a kind of suffocating positivity that can never produce what we ask of it. In essence, experience is about liberating us on the surface and yet tying us to the capitalist machine beneath. For some this is an emotional enterprise; it's about using emotion to heighten productivity (Han, 2017). For others it is a psychic one (McGowan, 2016) insofar as consumers locate themselves in a constant state of sublime dissatisfaction. McGowan goes on to argue that an overriding characteristic of a capitalist society is thus its ability to maintain its own constituency via a perpetual state of longing:

> Capitalism functions effectively as it does because it provides satisfaction for its subjects while at the same time hiding the awareness of this satisfaction from them. If we recognized that we obtained satisfaction from the failure to obtain the perfect commodity rather than from a wholly successful purchase, we would be freed from the psychic appeal of capitalism. That is not to say that we would never buy another commodity, but just that we would do so without a psychic investment in the promise of the commodity. (McGowan, 2016: 14)

It is my contention that through this perpetual sense of longing the psychological and thus the ideological power of consumption is strengthened and intensified. And as I suggested above, it is intensified momentarily: how we consume in the experience society gives us an incredible sense of control, simultaneously annexing such a sense of control only to take it away. Ironically, the more we come to envisage the world in which we live as our own – the more we try to wring as much experience out of it as we can – the less it belongs to us. At one level this is about the consumer committing to the kind of selfhood that excessive experiences of consumption imply, what Han calls the 'unfreedom of labour' which ultimately does nothing more than maximising capital while ensuring that the consumer is in thrall to it.

Capitalism and Social Change

This brings us back to the historical element of how capitalism has reinvented itself in the context of social change. The above process is made possible by the increasingly spectacular nature of consumption that builds upon the kinds of shifts I discussed above. Thus Hetherington (2007) focuses on the evolution of the relationship between the spectacle and consumer capitalism. He argues that by the beginning of the twenty-first century we 'have all ... become modern consuming spectators mirrored as subjects in what we buy' (2007: 26). The nature of the spectacle is evolving, the debate being to do with how passive the apparently manipulated consumer of the spectacle may or may not be. Have consumers moved on from their status as mere subjects vulnerable to festishistic forms of consumption? For Hetherington, modernity served to transform the nature of experience from that of tradition, memory and custom to a fragmentary set of experiences or events. What is interesting here is the suggestion that during the course of modernity experience came to be associated with a sense of loss; a loss of tradition, community, authenticity and the like in which consumption plays a key role. Above all perhaps, this is about a total separation between a lived reality and its representation, so that spectacle operates as an image-driven mode of mediation (Hetherington, 2007). But the danger here, as I pointed out in Chapter 1, is that what this all adds up to, especially in the context of Debord's (1995) work, is actually a denial of individual autonomy. The primary matter for debate, therefore, is the extent to which social reality is masked by the spectacular. How far has the spectacular comes to take on the character of that reality, and at what cost to the individual? Hetherington goes on to argue that the individual simultaneously possesses and is possessed by the commodity. Experience is both fragmented and manipulated and subject to a multiple range of meanings and interpretations. But how does the experience society affect this balance?

From a critical perspective there has long been a perceived, albeit unspoken, danger in implying that consumption is somehow inherently passive: almost as if it is something that we suffer or escape *from*. Indeed, it has been argued that those of a Marxist or critical persuasion find it difficult to engage with what consumption actually means to consumers precisely because to do so would put them in the invidious position of condemning the act of consumption itself (Miles, 2012; Ray and Sayer, 1999a). To do so would imply that working-class consumers in particular, who may have limited resources but yet are under significant pressure to be seen as citizens of such a society, are not only passive, but docile acolytes easily seduced by the promises that the experience society makes.

What is certain, and however extreme the position of authors such as Horkheimer and Adorno (1972) might be, power relations are nonetheless clearly expressed through the mechanisms that the market produces (Ray and Sayer, 1999b). And yet for too long sociological approaches to consumption have tended to shy away from seeing consumption through a critical lens. The recent dominance of practice theory within the realms of consumer studies is evidence enough of the dangers of a critically inert research agenda (see Warde, 2005). In fact it has never been more important to engage with consumption in a wholeheartedly critical fashion that embraces the notion that in some shape or form the market continues to mould the self in increasingly subtle ways. It is also important to remember, as Tuan (1982) notes in his broader discussion of experience, that what and how we experience is perhaps most importantly a product of feeling and thought, and as such is something we create, or at least that we feel we can create. This last point is particularly significant, as my argument is that although consumers are beholden to a system and a way of life defined for them by consumer capitalism, what is distinctive about that world today is, ironically, its ability to provide the consumer with the sense that within these boundaries there are boundless opportunities for the exploration of a selfhood: that the self is perhaps freer than ever before.

But ultimately we are kidding nobody but ourselves. As Margolis (1998) suggests, the world of market exchange is inherently unstable, and therefore as individuals all we are actually doing is building 'high and stable boundaries around ourselves and our feelings so that, to a large degree, the purpose of all activities, all buying and selling, is to bring us pleasant emotions and help us avoid unpleasant emotions' (1998: 141). In this sense the evolution of consumer capitalism is inevitably all about the way it has managed to surround its citizens with a cocoon that protects the consumer from thoughts of their own non-consumerist fallibility. Consumer capitalism can continue to thrive insofar as it convinces the consumer that he or she is free to create feeling and thought around the experiences they consume.

The experience society has succeeded in putting self-narratives at the heart of the capitalist mission. This is not something that has happened overnight, rather it is the position it has been moving towards ever since the first Model T Ford rolled off the production line. But as the subtitle of this book also suggests, in its own way it also constitutes a significant change of direction that accommodates the increasing sophistication of consumers, or at least their ability to use what they consume thoughtfully and strategically. It is important to remember that consumers are more sophisticated today than they have ever been before. What consumer capitalism does under the guise of the experience society is to utilise the very narcissistic drive it has spent decade after decade fostering, combining that with a more reflexive form of criticality, while creating in combination a self more compliant to the world of commodified experience than ever before.

The individual is no longer who or what they consume, but rather what narrative they present to the world about how and what they consume. In effect, in an experience society we have become flâneurs of the self. Consumer capitalism has obliged us to sieve the world through how we can better understand and thus promote our best self-interest. Our pleasure resides not in observing others, but in of taking a step out of ourselves, in order to understand how we can best be, and more importantly *feel*, ourselves through the opportunities that consumer capitalism provides for us to bloom. Another way of describing this might be to say that consumer capitalism has resolved the problem of the fragmented self. In discussions around post-modernity, commentators long debated the instable, incoherent, self-directed nature of the self; it's ability to reinvent itself from one moment to the next (Featherstone, 1991). This brought with it challenges, not least as regards a preoccupation with defining consumers as marketable subsets: the notion that by knowing your consumer you can market to them in a more effective fashion. If the self had become self-defined and was no longer the product of tradition, loyalty and a commitment to fashions located in the social, how could consumer capitalism control its markets and maximise spend in the process? The answer lies in experience.

The experience society constructs a world for us in which we are in the hunt for constant exceptionalism. We seek novelty and excitement, but we do so in the name of maximising our own possibilities (Garcia, 2018). There is a danger in this: the danger of burn out. But we are saved from such a state of affairs by the fact that the experience society is in the business of constantly reinventing experience to the extent that all experiences are ultimately as routine and predictable as that which the consumer originally sought his or her escape (Garcia, 2018). The power of consumer capitalism lies in its continual ability to use the self as a conduit by which the more routine such experiences becomes the less routine and the more personally fulfilling they feel. The irony is that the diner no longer has to be satisfied with the menu. Today's consumer is a more reflexive consumer, but he or she is no less subject to the determinism of capitalism as a result. Žižek (2014) describes a process that could be defined as *jouissance*, in which the more you consume a product the more it is lacking and the guiltier you feel for consuming it (see also Cremin, 2011). The consumer is encouraged to desire particular psychic emollients, and this is achieved by an emptying out of fetishised content so that a lack of content is effectively presented up for consumption. The consumer is obliged to enjoy; to desire not just a product but desire itself (Žižek, 2014). He or she is thus effectively satisfied by the partial satisfactions that consumer capitalism provides, for at that moment the experience of being on the cusp of a fulfilled desire is as satisfying as consumer capitalism gets. The consumer does not need to be fully satisfied; to be so would constitute a counterproductive state: he or she is conditioned into maximising the moments in which satisfaction can nearly, but never, be achieved.

Conclusion

My analysis is the product of a particular way of looking at the world. It is the artefact of a particular perspective that I would argue has roots in my upbringing in an aspirational working-class family that saw success as being defined by the kind of house in which you lived and whether or not you had a new enough car on the drive. Through that experience I bring to my analysis certain expectations, presuppositions and no doubt a whole raft of class biases and forebodings. My understanding of the experience society also takes into account a broader historical shift towards the collapsing of the public and the private (Curtis, 2013), so that the personal is increasingly exposed and thus more vulnerable to what consumer capitalism asks of it.

My acknowledgement of the above leads me to reflect briefly on what my analysis seeks to achieve, and specifically on Illouz's (2007: 95) contention that, 'in order to criticize a cultural practice, the cultural critic ought to use the moral criteria at work within the community (or social sphere) she or he is critiquing'. To put this another way, Illouz calls for a critical approach capable of balancing an understanding of the ways in which particular cultural practices further, in this case, the consumer's needs and desires, in such a way that it transcends the cultural critics' fondness for political predisposition. In this way any sense of what can emancipate, or perhaps what might simply offer a modicum of hope, can emerge from social practice itself, rather than from a skewed way of seeing the world and its toils. From this perspective we could argue that the life that the experience society offers is not entirely, either personally or emotionally, impoverished, but rather that it impressively expands the avenues of sociability by which the individual can locate and revitalise his or her selfhood. The experience society is underpinned by a set of conditions that are not so fragmented that they are alienating, but rather that have become so customary that they are simply *too* common. In short, we are all experiencing the experience society in ways that feel to us, as sovereign individuals, as though they are entirely unique. And yet, what they ultimately do is demonstrate consumer capitalism's ability to provide a common framework which propels us into a world of reverential self-conception. Illouz (2007: 112) perhaps sums this up most effectively in the following two sentences:

The psychological persuasion has transformed the terms of this duality between a private moral self and a public amoral instrumental strategic conduct. For ... the private and public spheres have become intertwined with each other, each mirroring the other, absorbing each other's mode of action and justification, and ensuring that instrumental reason be used in and applied to the realm of emotions and conversely, making self-realization and the claim to a full emotional life become the compass of instrumental reason.

The question Illouz asks is whether or not the above state of affairs offers us a greater degree of agency. For Illouz our experience of the world is the product of a split between a commodified and rationalised selfhood and a private world dominated by self-generated fantasy. In the entirety of this experience the economic and the romantic are increasingly difficult to separate. The experience society allows us to explore romantic notions of fulfilled selfhood. Experiences are the means by which consumer capitalism is able to engineer our sense of satisfaction.

But ultimately, even fantasy is controlled by a market definition of what such fantasies should be.

It's on the above basis that we find ourselves at a turning point in history. At a time when voices for the tempering of consumption seek to establish themselves as a focal point for ongoing environmental outrage, we can conclude that consumer capitalism's powers of persuasion are ever more sophisticated. They are capable of enticing the self in ways that not even Schulze (1995) could have predicted. For consumer capitalism persuades us that any answers to our daily travails lie within *ourselves* and not within the broader social, economic and cultural contexts which framed them. It's in this way that mindfulness is indicative of how the destructive logic of contemporary capitalism is perpetuated. The experience society is a society that effectively sells our selves back to us. And in this sense the possibility of reinvention, of our grasping a post-consumer future, are perhaps further away than ever before.

By way of reaching my end point I would like to refer back to the single quotation that around 25 years ago propelled my own academic journey into the experience of consumerism as a way of life (Miles, 1998):

> the conditions of everyday social intercourse, in societies based on mass production and mass consumption, encourage an unprece-dented attention to superficial impressions and images, to the point where the self becomes almost indistinguishable from its surface. (Lasch, 1984: 30)

The notion that consumer capitalism had created a new kind of self – the product of a world in which the spectacularly superficial could undermine and reinvent what it meant to be you or me – remains a vivid one. But what Lasch describes is no longer tenable. His descrip-tion of selfhood is one of vulnerability, and almost of betrayal. A self propped up by a system that has apparently, long ago, lost faith in what it means to be human. This is not the experience society. The expe-rience society revels in the reactivation of selfhood: it is stronger and more resilient, but its resilience continues to flounder on false promises. Meanwhile, consumer capitalism continues to thrive on its ability to put the self at the centre of the consumer's imaginary as a way of dislodging the uncertainties and anxieties of social change in favour of momentary consummations of consumption. The self has been rebooted. And on this basis I conclude with a key sentence of my own, borrowed at least in part from Lasch himself:

> The conditions of everyday social intercourse, in societies based on mass production and mass consumption, encourage an unprecedented attention to the experiential maximisation of selfhood, to the point where consumer capitalism becomes almost indistinguishable from the carpe diem of its surface.

The world that this creates for us is a world in which we are simultaneously more sophisticated in our understanding of how consumer capitalism can control us, and yet ever more vulnerable to the sophisticated ways in which it does so. The experience society is a society in which the perplexing realities of how consumer capitalism operates are close to the surface of our everyday lives. Any sense of our liberation is meaningless insofar as it simply perpetuates a mindset in which the self reigns. But at least it is closer to the surface.

To end on a positive note, it is possible that consumer capitalism contains the seeds of its own destruction after all. And perhaps the more we seek to live in the moment, the more we shall realise that, in such moments, personal insurrections arise. Only then can we move beyond a future that compels us to experience nothing more than a self borne of choices, freedoms and menus maladroit.

References

Abercrombie, N. and Longhurst, B. (1998) *Audiences: A Sociological Theory of Performance and Imagination*, London: Sage.

Adorno, T. (1975) Culture industry reconsidered, *New German Critique*, 6: 12–19.

Adorno, T. (1989) The culture industry reconsidered, in S. Bronner and D. Kellner (eds) *Critical Theory and Society: A Reader*, London: Routledge.

Adorno, T. (1991a) *The Culture Industry: Selected Essays on Mass Culture*, London: Routledge.

Adorno, T. (1991b) On the fetish character in music and the regression of listening, in *The Culture Industry Reconsidered: Selected Essays on Mass Culture*, London: Routledge.

Aiello, G. and Dickinson, G. (2014) Beyond authenticity: a visual-material analysis of locality in the global redesign of Starbuck stores, *Visual Communication*, 13(3), 303–21.

Aldridge, J. (2019) Starbucks smells the coffee, *Sunday Times*, 12 April: 6.

Andrews, D. L. (2006) Disneyization, Debord, and the integrated NBA spectacle, *Social Semiotics*, 16(1), 89–102.

Andrews, D. L. (2008) Sport, culture and late capitalism, in B. Carrington and I. McDonald (eds) *Marxism, Cultural Studies and Sport*, London: Routledge.

Augé, M. (1995) *Non-Places: Introduction to an Anthropology of Supermodernity*, London: Verso Books.

Bakhtin, M. (1984) *Problems of Dostoevsky's Poetics*, Minneapolis: University of Minnesota Press.

Baudrillard, J. (1991) *Seduction*, New York: St. Martin's Press.

Bauman, Z. (1998) *Work, Consumerism and the New Poor*, Buckingham: Open University Press.

Beal, B. and Wilson, C. (2004) 'Chicks dig scars': commercialisation and the transformations of skateboarders' identities, in B. Wheaton (ed.) *Understanding Lifestyle Sports*, London: Routledge.

Beck, U. (1992) *Risk Society: Towards a New Modernity*, London: Sage.

Beck, U. (2000) *The Brand New World of Work*, Cambridge: Polity Press.

Begout, B. (2003) *Zeropolis: The Experience of Las Vegas*, London: Reaktion.

Belk, R. W. (2013) Extended self in a digital world, *Journal of Consumer Research*, 40(3), 477–500.

Belk, R. W. (2014) Digital consumption and the extended self, *Journal of Marketing Management*, 30(11–12), 1101–18.

Bell, D. (1973) *The Coming of Post-Industrial Society*, New York: Basic Books.

Bell, E. (2008) *Theories of Performance*, London: Sage.

Benjamin, W. (2005a) *Selected Writings 1913–26*, Volume 1, London: Belknap Press.

Benjamin, W. (2005b) *Selected Writings 1927–1930*, Volume 2, Cambridge, MA: Harvard University Press.

Benjamin, W. (2008) [1936] The work of art in the age of technological reproducibility: third version, in H. Eiland, B. Doherty and T. Levin (eds) *The Work of Art in the Age of its Technological Reproducibility and Other Writings on Media*, Cambridge: MA.: Harvard University Press.

Benson, C. (1993) *Absorbed Self: Pragmatism, Psychology and Aesthetic Experience*, London: Prentice-Hall.

Berardi, F. (2009) *The Soul at Work: From Alienation to Autonomy*, New York: Semiotext(e).

Betancourt, M. (2015) *The Critique of Digital Capitalism: An Analysis of the Political Economy of Digital Culture and Technology*, New York: Punctum Books.

Bishop, C. (2004) Antagonism and relational aesthetics, *October*, 110(Fall), 51–79.

Blackshaw, T. and Crabbe, T. (2004) *New Perspectives on Sport and 'Deviance': Consumption, Performativity and Social Control*, London: Routledge.

Borges, S., Ehmann, S. and Klanten, R. (2013) *Work Scape: New Spaces for New Work*, Berlin: Die Gestalten Verlag.

Bourdieu, P. (1986) *Distinction: A Social Critique of the Judgement of Taste*, London: Routledge.

Brohm, J.-M. (1978) *Sport: A Prison of Measure Time*, London: Inks Links.

Brown, W. (2015) *Undoing the Demos: Neoliberalism's Stealth Revolution*, New York: Zone Books.

Brown, M. (2019) Tate Modern beat British Museum to become most visited tourist attraction in UK, *The Guardian*, 27 March.

Buck-Morris, S. (1992) Aesthetics and anaesthetics: Walter Benjamin's artwork essay reconsidered, *October*, 62, 3–41.

Bull, M. (2007) *Sound Moves: iPod Culture and Urban Experience*, London: Routledge.

Burgess, J. and Green, J. (2013) *YourTube: Online Video and Participatory Culture*, Cambridge: Polity Press.

Butler, J. (2008) Performativity, precarity and sexual politics, in *AIBR: Revista de Antropología Iberoamericana*, 4(3), i–xiii.

Butsch, R. (1990) Introduction: leisure and hegemony, in R. Butsch (ed.) *For Fun and Profit: The Transformation of Leisure into Consumption*, Philadelphia: Temple University Press.

Cameron, A. (2018) *Affected Labour in a Café Culture: The Atmospheres and Economics of 'Hip' Melbourne*, London: Routledge.

Campbell, C. (1987) *The Romantic Ethic and the Spirit of Modern Consumerism*, Oxford: Wiley-Blackwell.

Carrington, B. and McDonald, I. (2008) Marxism, cultural studies and sport: mapping the field, in B. Carrington and I. McDonald (eds) *Marxism, Cultural Studies and Sport*, London: Routledge.

Cashmore, E. (2014) *Celebrity Culture*, 2nd edition, London: Routledge.

Castells, M. (1996) *The Rise of the Network Society: The Information Age: Economy, Society and Culture*, Volume 1, Oxford: Wiley-Blackwell.

Chaplin, S. and Holding, E. (1998) Consuming Architecture, in *Architectural Design: Consuming Architecture*, Cambridge: John Wiley & Sons.

Chen, C. P. (2016) Forming digital self and parasocial relationships on YouTube, *Journal of Consumer Culture*, 16(1), 232–54.

Clark, T. (2008) *Starbucked: A Double Tall Tale of Caffeine, Commerce and Culture*, London: Sceptre.

Clegg, J. and Robinson, J. (2018) *The Club: How the Premier League Became the Richest, Most Disruptive Business in Sport*, London: John Murray.

Coates, D. (1995) *Running the Country*, London: Hodder and Stoughton.

Cohen, S. (2010) Searching for escape, authenticity and identity: experiences of 'lifestyle travellers', in M. Morgan, P. Lugosi and J. R. Brent Richie (eds) *The Tourism and Leisure Experience: Consumer and Management Perspectives*, Bristol: Channel View.

Collareo, P. L. (2003) The sociology of the self, *Annual Review of Sociology*, 29, 115–33.

Conn, D. (2018) Analysis: football remains the battering ram to retain supporter's affections, *The Guardian*, 15 February.

Craib, C. (1998) *Experiencing Identity*, London: Sage.

Crawford, G. (2004) *Consuming Sport: Fans, Sport and Culture*, London: Routledge.

Cremin, C. (2011) *Capitalism's New Clothes: Enterprise, Ethics and Enjoyment in Times of Crisis*, London: Pluto.

Csikzentmihalyi, M. (2002) *Finding Flow: The Psychology Of Engagement With Everyday Life*, New York: Rider.

Curtis, N. (2013) *Idiotism: Capitalism and the Privatisation of Life*, London: Pluto.

Cutright, K. M., Samper, A. and Fitzsimons, G. J. (2013) We are what we buy? In A. A. Ruvio and Russel W. Belk (eds) *The Routledge Companion to Identity and Consumption*, London: Routledge.

Davis, S. (1997) *Spectacular Nature: Corporate Culture and the Sea World Experience*, London: University of California Press.

Debord, G. (1995) *The Society of the Spectacle*, New York: Zone Books.

Denegri-Knott, J. and Molesworth, M. (2012) Introduction to digital virtual consumption, in M. Molesworth and J. Denegri-Knott (eds) *Digital Virtual Consumption*, London: Routledge.

Dewey, J. (2005) *Art as Experience*, New York: Perigee Books.

Dickinson, G. (2002) Joes' rhetoric: finding authenticity at Starbucks, *Rhetoric Society Quarterly*, 32 (4), 5–27.

Dittmar, H. (2010) *Consumer Culture, Identity and Well-Being*, Hove: Psychology Press.

Du Gay, P., Hall, S., Janes, L., Mackay, H. and Negus, K. (1996) *Doing Cultural Studies: The Story of the Sony Walkman*, London: Sage.

Dumazedier, J. (1967) *Toward a Society of Leisure*, London: Collier-Macmillan.

Dunn, R. G. (2008) *Identifying Consumption: Subjects and Objects in Contemporary Society*, Philadelphia: Temple University Press.

Dyckhoff, T. (2017) *The Age of Spectacle: Adventures in Architecture and the 21st-Century City*, London: Random Books.

Edwards, T. (2000) *Contradictions of Consumption: Concepts, Practices and Politics in Consumer Society*, Buckingham: Open University Press.

Elias, N. (2008) *Quest for Excitement: Sport and Leisure in the Civilising Process*, Collected Works of Norbert Elias, Dublin: University College Dublin Press.

Elliot, A. (2013) *Concepts of the Self*, Cambridge: Polity.

Elliot, A. (2015) *Identity Troubles*, London: Routledge.

Ellis, M. (2004) *The Coffee House: A Cultural History*, London: Phoenix.

Farokhmanesh, M. (2018) YouTube is the preferred platform of today's teens, *The Verge*, 31 May, www.theverge.com/2018/5/31/17382058/youtube-teens-preferred-platform. Accessed 15 November 2019.

Featherstone, M. (1991) *Consumer Culture and Postmodernism*, London: Sage.

Fellner, K. (2008) *Wrestling with Starbucks: Conscience, Capital, Cappuccino*, London: Rutgers University Press.

Fernandez-Galiano, L. (2005) Spectacle and its discontents; or, the elusive joys of architainment, in W. S. Saunders (ed.) *Commodification and Spectacle in Architecture, Harvard Design Magazine Reader*, Minneapolis: University of Minnesota Press.

Fiske, J. (1989) *Understanding Popular Culture*, London: Routledge.

Fiske, J. (1992) The cultural economy of fandom, in L. Lewis (ed.) *The Adoring Audience: Fan Culture and Popular Media*, London: Routledge.

Foley, M. (2011) *The Age of Absurdity: Why Modern Life Makes It Hard to Be Happy*, London: Simon and Schuster.

Forde, E. (2019) How Naspster freed music, *The Guardian*, 31 May.

Freud, S. (1920) *Beyond the Pleasure Principle, Group Psychology and Other Works: The Standard Edition of the Complete Psychological Works of Sigmund Freud*, Volume 18, London: Vintage.

Gabriel, Y. and Lang, T. (2016) *The Unmanageable Consumer*, 3rd edition, London: Sage.

Gallagher, L. (2017) *The Airbnb Story*, London: Virgin Books.

Gandini, A. (2015) Digital work: self-branding and social capital in the freelance knowledge economy, *Marketing Theory*, 16(1), 123–41.

Garcia, T. (2018) *The Life Intense: A Modern Obsession*, Edinburgh: Edinburgh University Press.

Geoghegan, J. (2018) Fashion suffers sharpest sales decline in nine years, *Drapers*, 9 May.

Giddens, A. (1983) *Profiles and Critiques in Social Theory*, Berkeley, University of California Press.

Giddens, A. (1991) *Modernity and Self-Identity*, Cambridge: Polity.

Giroux, H. (2014) *The Violence of Organized Forgetting: Thinking Beyond America's Disimagination Machine*, San Francisco, CA: City Lights.

Giulianotti, R. (2002) Supporters, followers, fans, and flaneurs: a taxonomy of spectator identities in football, *Journal of Sport and Social Issues*, 26(1), 25–46.

Giulianotti, R. (2011) Sport mega events, urban football carnivals and securitised commodification: the case of the English Premier League, *Urban Studies*, 489(15), 3291–310.

Gorz, A. (1967) *Strategy for Labour: A Radical Proposal*, Boston: Beacon Press.

Gorz, A. (1999) *Reclaiming Work: Beyond the Wage-Based Society*, Cambridge: Polity Press.

Gottdiener, M. (2001) *The Theming Of America: American Dreams, Media Fantasies, and Themed Environments*, London: Routledge.

Goulding, C. (1999) Contemporary museum culture and consumer behaviour, *Journal of Marketing Management*, 15(7), 647–71.

Govers, R. and Go, F. (2009) *Place Branding: Glocal, Virtual, and Physical Identities Constructed, Imagined and Experienced*, Basingstoke: Palgrave Macmillan.

Gramsci, A. (2005) *Selections from the Prison Notebooks of Antonio Gramsci*, edited and translated by Q. Hoare and G. Nowell Smith, London: Lawrence & Wishart.

Gratton, L. (2014) *The Shift: The Future of Work is Already Here*, London: HarperCollins.

Greif, M. (2017) *Against Everything: On Dishonest Times*, London: Verso.

Grinshpun, H. (2014) Deconstructing a global commodity: coffee, culture, and consumption in Japan, *Journal of Consumer Culture*, 14(3), 343–64.

Han, B. C. (2017) *Psychopolitics: Neoliberalism and New Technologies of Power*, London: Verso.

Hankiss, E. (2006) *The Toothpaste of Immortality: Self-construction in the Consumer Age*, Washington, DC: Johns Hopkins University Press.

Hannigan, J. (2005) *Fantasy City: Pleasure and Profit in the Postmodern Metropolis*, London: Routledge.

Hartmann, J. (2011) Starbucks and the third wave, in S. F. Parker and M. W. Dawson (eds) *Coffee – Philosophy for Everyone: Grounds for Debate*, Oxford: Wiley-Blackwell.

Harvey, D. (1989) From managerialism to entrepreneurialism: the transformation in urban governance in late capitalism, *Geografiska Annaler, Series B. Human Geography*, 71(1), 3–17.

Harvey, D. (1990) *The Condition of Postmodernity*, Oxford: Blackwell.

Hayward, K. (2004) *City Limits: Crime, Consumer Culture and the Urban Experience*, London: Glasshouse Press.

Heath, J. and Potter, A. (2005) *The Rebel Sell: How the Counterculture Became Consumer Culture*, Chichester: Capstone.

Hebdige, M. (1989) *Subculture: The Meaning of Style*, London: Routledge.

Hedges, C. (2009) *Empire of Illusion: The End of Literacy and the Triumph of Spectacle*, New York: Nation Books.

Herwig, O. and Holzherr, F. (2005) *Dream Worlds: Architecture and Entertainment*, London: Prestel.

Hetherington, K. (2007) *Capitalism's Eye: Cultural Spaces of the Commodity*, London: Routledge.

Holland, R. (1977) *Self and Social Context*, Basingstoke: Macmillan.

Horkheimer, M. and Adorno, T. W. (1972) *Dialectic of Enlightenment*, London: Allen Lane.

Horne, J. (2006) *Sport in Consumer Culture*, Buckingham: Palgrave.

Horne, J. and Whannel, G. (2012) *Understanding the Olympics*, London: Routledge.

Hughson, J., Inglis, D. and Free, M. (2005) *The Uses of Sport: A Critical Study*, London: Routledge.

Hurley, A. (2001) *Diners, Bowling Alleys and Trailer Parks: Chasing the American Dream in Postwar Consumer Culture*, New York: Basic Books.

Illouz, E. (2007) *Cold Intimacies: The Making of Emotional Capitalism*, Cambridge: Polity.

Illouz, E. (2009) Emotions, imagination and consumption: a new research agenda, *Journal of Consumer Culture*, 3(9), 377–413.

Jafari, A, Taheri, B. and vom Lehn, D. (2013) Cultural consumption, interactive sociality, and the museum, *Journal of Marketing Management*, 29(15–16), 1729–52.

Jameson, F. (1991) *Postmodernism, or, the Cultural Logic of Late Capitalism*, London: Verso.

Jameson, F. (2007) *Jameson on Jameson: Conversations with Cultural Marxism*, edited by Ian Buchanan, London: Duke University Press.

Jappe, A. (1999) *Guy Debord*, London: University of California Press.

Jay, M. (2005) *Songs of Experience: Modern American and European Variations on a Universal Theme*, London: University of California Press.

Jeffries, S. (2016) *Grand Hotel Abyss: The Lives of the Frankfurt School*, London: Verso.

Jensen, R. (1999) *The Dream Society: How the Coming Shift from Information to Imagination Will Transform Your Business*, London: McGraw-Hill.

Jones, P. (2011) *The Sociology of Architecture: Constructing Identities*, Liverpool: Liverpool University Press.

Jones, T. (2019) Analysis, *The Observer*, 6 January.

Kelliher, C. and Anderson, A. (2010) Doing more with less? Flexible working practices and the intensification of work, *Human Relations*, 3(1), 83–106.

Kellner, D. (2003) *Media Spectacle*, London: Routledge.

Khondker, H. H. and Robertson, R. (2018) Glocalization, consumption, and cricket: the Indian Premier League, *Journal of Consumer Culture*, 18(2), 279–97.

Klingmann, A. (2007) *Brandscapes: Architecture in the Experience Economy*, London: MIT Press.

Klonk, C. (2009) *Spaces of Experience: Art Gallery Interiors from 1800 to 2000*, London: Yale University Press.

Knorr Cetina, K. (2001) Postsocial relations: theorizing sociality in a postsocial environment, in G. Ritzer and B. Smart (eds) *Handbook of Social Theory*, London: Sage.

Kolberg, S. (2016) Constructing a 'democratic' dreamworld: carnival cruise ships and an aesthetic of optimism, *Journal of Consumer Culture*, 16(1), 3–21.

Koolhaas, R. (2008) In search of authenticity, in R. Burdett and D. Sudjic (eds) *The Endless City*, London: Phaidon.

Krauss, R. (1990) The cultural logic of the late capitalist museum, *October*, 54, 3–17.

Kreiss, D., Finn, M. and Turner, F. (2011) The limits of peer production: some reminders from Max Weber for the network society, *New Media and Society*, 13(2), 243–59.

Krier, D. and Swart, W. (2016) *Sturgis and the New Economy of Spectacle*, Chicago: Haymarket Books.

Kulkarni, N. and Joseph-Lester, J. (2004) *Disorientation and Spectacle in Retail Architecture*, London: Artswords Press.

Kurylo, B. (2018) Technologised consumer culture: the Adorno–Benjamin debate and the reverse side of politicisation, *Journal of Consumer Culture*, 17, 1–18.

Lampugnani, V. M. (2010) Insight versus entertainment: untimely meditations on the architecture of twentieth century art museums, in S. Macdonald (ed.) *A Companion to Museum Studies*, Cambridge: Blackwell.

Landry, C. (2006) *The Art of City Making*, London: Earthscan.

Lasch, C. (1979) *The Culture of Narcissism: American Life in an Age of Diminishing Expectations*, New York: W. W. Norton.

Lasch, C. (1984) *The Minimal Self: Psychic Survival in Troubled Times*, New York: Picador.

Lash, S. (2018) *Experience: New Foundations for the Human Sciences*, Cambridge: Polity Press.

Lazzarato, M. (2006) Immaterial Labour, in M. Hardt and P. Virno (eds) *Radical Thought in Italy: A Potential Politics*, Minneapolis: University of Minnesota Press.

Leary, M. and Tangney, J. P. (2012) The self as an organizing construct in the behavioural and social sciences, in M. Leary and J. P. Tangney, *Handbook of Self and Identity*, 2nd edition, London: The Guildford Press.

Lehdonvirta, V. (2012) A history of the digitalization of consumer culture, in M. Molesworth and J. Denegri-Knott (eds) *Digital Virtual Consumption*, London: Routledge.

Lifton, R. J. (1995) *The Protean Self: Human Resilience in an Age of Fragmentation*, London: University of Chicago Press.

Lodziak, C. (1995) *Manipulating Needs: Capitalism and Culture*, London: Pluto Press.

Lodziak, C. (2002) *The Myth of Consumerism*, London: Pluto Press.

Lonsway, B. (2009) *Making Leisure Work: Architecture and the Experience Economy*, London: Routledge.

Lukas, S. A. (2008) *Theme Park*, New York: Reaktion Books.

Lukas, S. A. (ed.) (2016) *A Reader in Themed and Immersive Spaces*, Carnegie Mellon: ETC Press.

Lukes, S. A. (2005) *Power: A Radical View*, 2nd edition, New York: Palgrave Macmillan.

MacCannell, D. (1999) *The Tourist: A New Theory of the Leisure Class*, London: University of California Press.

MacInnes, P. (2018) Game's bubble showing no sign of bursting, *The Guardian*, 26 January.

Macleod, S., Austin, T., Hale, J. and Hing-Kay, O. H. (eds) (2018) *The Future of Museum and Gallery Design: Purposes, Processes, Perception*, London: Routledge.

Maguire Smith, J. (2008) *Fit for Consumption, Sociology and the Business of Fitness*, London: Routledge.

MammaMia! (2019) What the audiences are saying: Mamma Mia! The Party at London's O2, www.youtube.com/watch?v=I16sWzjPCgk. Accessed 15 November 2019.

Manzenreiter, W. (2006) Sport spectacles, uniformities and the search for identity in late modern Japan, *The Sociological Review*, 54(2), 114–59.

Manzo, L. (2003) Beyond house and haven: toward a revisioning of the emotional relationships with places, *Journal of Environmental Psychology*, 23(1), 47–61.

Margolis, D. R. (1998) *The Fabric of Self: A Theory of Ethic and Emotions*, London: Yale University Press.

Massumi, B. (2015) *The Power at the End of the Economy*, London: Duke University Press.

McCarthy, J. and Wright, P. P. (2004) *Technology as Experience*, Cambridge, MA: MIT Press.

McGowan, T. (2016) *Capitalism and Desire: The Psychic Cost of Free Markets*, New York: Columbia University Press.

Marcuse, H. (1986) *Reason and Revolution*, London: Routledge.

Marcuse, H. (2002) *One-Dimensional Man: Studies in the Ideology of Advanced Industrial Society*, London: Routledge.

Marx, K. (1989) *Grundrisse: Foundations Of The Critique Of Political Economy (Revised)*, London: Penguin Books.

McCannell, D. (1989) *The Tourist: A New Theory of the Leisure Class*, New York: Schocken.

McCurry, J. (2018) Japan tourism backlash: new law targets Airbnb as visitor numbers up 250%, *The Guardian*, 16 June.

Melucci, A. (1996) *The Playing Self: Person and Meaning in the Planetary Society*, Cambridge: Cambridge University Press.

Miles, S. (1998) *Consumerism as a Way of Life*, London: Sage.

Miles, S. (2007) Consumption as freedom: intergenerational relationships in a changing China, in J. Powell and I. Cook (eds) *New Perspectives on Ageing in China*, New York: Nova.

Miles, S. (2012) The neoliberal city and the pro-active complicity of the citizen consumer, *Journal of Consumer Culture*, 12, 216–30.

Miles, S. (2016) Flawed theming: Center Parcs as a commodified utopia, in Scott A. Lukas (ed.) *A Reader in Themed and Immersive Spaces*, New York: ETC Press.

Miles, S. (2019) Immersive narratives of 'self-work' in an experience society: understanding the cruise ship experience, *Leisure Studies* 38(4), 523–34.

Miller, D. and Woodward, S. (2012) *Blue Jeans: The Art of the Ordinary*, London: University of California Press.

Miller, T. (2009) Michel Foucault and the critique of sport, in B. Carrington and I. Macdonald (eds) *Marxism, Cultural Studies and Sport*, London: Routledge.

Mitrasinovic, M. (2006) *Total Landscape, Theme Parks, Public Space*, Aldershot: Ashgate.

Moccia, L., Mazza, M., Di Nicola, M. and Janiri, L. (2018) The experience of pleasure: a perspective between neuroscience and psychoanalysis, *Frontiers in Human Neuroscience*, 12, 359.

Molesworth, M. and Denegri-Knott, J. (2012) Conclusions: trajectories of digital virtual consumption, in M. Molesworth and J. Denegri-Knott (eds) *Digital Virtual Consumption*, London: Routledge.

Moore, P. (2018) *The Quantified Self in Precarity: Work, Technology and What Counts*, London: Routledge.

Moran, M. (2015) *Identity and Capitalism*, London: Sage.

Mort, F. (1989) The politics of consumption in S. Hall and M. Jacques (eds) *New Times: The Changing Face of Politics in the 1990s*, London: Lawrence and Wishart.

Moss, M. (2007) *Shopping as an Entertainment Experience*, Plymouth: Lexington Books.

Newell, S. (2012) *The Modernity Bluff: Crime, Consumption and Citizenship in Côte D'Ivoire*, Chicago: Chicago University Press.

Newhouse, V. (1998) *Towards a New Museum*, New York: Monacelli.

Newport, N. (2019) *Digital Minimalism: On Living Better with Less Technology*, London: Penguin.

Niedzviecki, H. (2006) *How Individuality became the New Conformity*, San Francisco, CA: City Lights.

Ockman, J. (2004) New politics of the spectacle: 'Bilbao' and the global imagination, in D. Medina Lasansky and B. McLaren (eds) *Architecture and Tourism: Perception, Performance and Place*, Oxford: Berg.

Oldenburg, R. (1989) *The Great Good Place*, Cambridge, CA: Capo Press.

O'Neill, J. (1999) Economy, equality and recognition, in L. Ray and A. Sayer (eds) *Culture and Economy after the Cultural Turn*, London: Sage.

O'Sullivan, E. and Spangler, K. (1999) *Experience Marketing: Strategies for the New Millennium*, London: Venture.

Papacharissi, Z. (2011) *A Networked Self: Identity, Community and Culture on Social Network Sites*, London: Routledge.

Pariser, E. (2011) *The Filter Bubble: What the Internet is Hiding from You*, New York: Penguin.

Paterson, M. (2006) *Consumption and Everyday Life*, London: Routledge.

Perelman, M. (2012) *Barbaric Sport: A Global Plague*, London: Verso.

Perkins, S. (1995) *Experience*, London: Booth-Clibborn.

Pettinger, L. (2016) *Work, Consumption and Capitalism*, Buckingham: Palgrave.

Pimlott, M. (2007) *Without and Within: Essays on Territory and the Interior*, New York: Episode.

Pine, B. J. and Gilmore, J. H. (1999) *The Experience Economy: Work is Theater and Every Business a Stage*, Cambridge, MA: Harvard Business Review Press.

Ploeg, A. J. (2017) Going global: fantasy sports gameplay paradigms, fan identities and cultural implications in an international context, *European Journal of Cultural Studies*, 20(6), 724–43.

Porat, B. (2012) From community to commodity: the commodification of football in Israel, *Soccer & Society*, 13(3), 443–57.

Poulter, S. (2018) From lager to latte! Huge rise in coffee shops could see them outnumber pubs across Britain by 2030, study finds, *Daily Mail*, 9 April, www.dailymail.co.uk/news/article-5596395/Huge-rise-coffee-shops-outnumber-pubs-Britain-2030-study-finds.html. Accessed 15 November 2019.

Purser, R. F. (2019) *McMindfulness: How Mindfulness Became the New Capitalist Spirituality*, London: Repeater Books

Putnam, R. (2000) *Bowling Alone: The Collapse and Revival of American Community*, London: Schuster.

Quinlan Cutler, S. and Carmichael, B. A. (2010) The dimensions of the tourist experience, in M. Morgan, P. Lugosi and J. R. Brent Richie (eds) *The Tourism and Leisure Experience: Consumer and Management Perspectives*, Bristol: Channel View.

Raisborough, J. (2011) *Lifestyle Media and the Formation of Self*, Basingstoke: Palgrave Macmillan.

Randall, W. L. (2015) *The Narrative Complexity of Ordinary Life*, Oxford: Oxford University Press.

Ransome, P. (1999) *Sociology and the Future of Work*, Aldershot: Ashgate.

Ransome, P. (2005) *Work, Consumption and Culture: Affluence and Social Change in the Twenty-First Century*, London: Sage.

Rattle, R. (2014) Imaging identity in the age of internet and communication technologies, in N. Mathur (ed.) *Consumer Culture, Modernity and Identity*, London: Routledge.

Ray, L. and Sayer, A. (eds) (1999a) *Culture and Economy after the Cultural Turn*, London: Sage.

Ray, L. and Sayer, A. (1999b) Introduction, in L. Ray and A. Sayer (eds) *Culture and Economy after the Cultural Turn*, London: Sage.

Rifkin, J. (2014) *The Zero Marginal Cost Society: The Internet of Things, the Collaborative Commons and the Eclipse of Capitalism*, Basingstoke: Palgrave Macmillan.

Ritzer, G. (1993) *The McDonaldization of Society*, London: Pine Forge.

Ritzer, G. and Jurgenson, N. (2010) Production, consumption, prosumption: the nature of capitalism in the age of the digital 'prosumer', *Journal of Consumer Culture*, 10(1), 13–36.

Robinson, T. P. (2014) *Café Culture in Pune: Being Young and Middle Class in Urban India*, Oxford: Oxford University Press.

Robinson, A. (2011) In theory Bakhtin: carnival against capital, carnival against power, *Ceasefire*, 9 September, https://ceasefiremagazine.co.uk/in-theory-bakhtin-2/. Accessed 15 November 2019.

Rockwell, D. with Mau, B. (2006) *Spectacle: An Optimist's Handbook*, London: Phaidon.

Rojek, C. (1994) *Ways of Escape: Modern Transformation in Leisure and Travel*, London: Rowman and Littlefield.

Rojek, C. (2010) *The Labour of Leisure: The Culture of Free Time*, London: Sage.

Rybas, N. (2012) Producing the self at the digital interface, in P. Hope Cheong, J. N. Martin and L. P. Macfadyen (eds) *New Media and Intercultural Communication: Identity, Community and Politics*, Oxford: Peter Lang.

Sack, R. D. (1992) *Place, Modernity, and the Consumer's World: A Relational Framework for Geographical Analysis*, New York: Johns Hopkins University.

Salecl, R. (2011) *The Tyranny of Choice*, Croydon: Profile Books.

Sandercock, L. (1998) Towards cosmopolis: utopia as a construction site, *Architectural Design: Consuming Architecture*, Cambridge: John Wiley & Sons.

Schultz, H. (1997) *Pour Your Heart Into It: How Starbucks Built a Company One Cup at a Time*, New York: Hypeirion.

Schulze, G. (1995) *Die Erlebnisgesellschaft: Kultursoziologie der Gegenwart*, New York: Campus Verlag.

Seabrook, J. (1988) *The Leisure Society*, Oxford: Basil Blackwell.

Selstad, L. (2007) The social anthropology of the tourist experience: exploring the 'middle role', *Scandinavian Journal of Hospitality and Tourism*, 7(1), 19–33.

Sennett, R. (1998) *The Corrosion of Character: The Personal Consequences of Work in the New Capitalism*, London: W. W. Norton.

Sennett, R. (2006) *The Culture of the New Capitalism*, London: Yale University Press.

Serota, S. (2000) *Experience or Interpretation: The Dilemma of Museums of Modern Art*, London: Thames and Hudson.

Seymour, R. (2019) *The Twittering Machine*, London: Indigo Press.

Sherry, J. R. (1998) *Servicescapes: The Concept of Place in Contemporary Markets*, New York: McGraw-Hill.

Shields, R. (2003) *The Virtual*, London: Routledge.

Simon, B. (2009) *Everything but the Coffee: Learning about America from Starbucks*, Berkeley: University of California Press.

Slater, D. (1997) *Consumer Culture and Modernity*, Cambridge: Polity.

Smart, B. (2005) *The Sport Star: Modern Sport and the Cultural Economy of Sporting Celebrity*, London: Sage.

Smithers, R. (2017) La la yellow, avocado and pink help to beat the blues in 2017, *The Guardian*, 12 October.

Sorokin, M. (1992) *Variations on a Theme Park: The New American City and the End of Public Space*, New York: Hill and Wang.

Southwood, I. (2011) *Non-Stop Inertia*, Alresford: Zero Books.

Spencer, D. (2016) *The Architecture of Neoliberalism: How Contemporary Architecture Became an Instrument of Control and Compliance*, London: Bloomsbury.

Stebbins, R. A. (2009) *Leisure and Consumption: Common Ground/Separate Worlds*, Basingstoke: Palgrave Macmillan.

Stenner, P. (2017) *Liminality and Experience: A Transdisciplinary Approach to the Psychosocial*, London: Palgrave Macmillan.

Sternberg, E. (1999) *The Economy of Icons: How Business Manufactures Meanings*, London: Praeger.

Stone, M. (2015) Teens love YouTube because it makes them feel good about themselves, a new survey says, *Business Insider*, 3 March, www.business insider.com/teens-love-youtube-because-it-makes-them-feel-good-about-themselves-2015-3?r=US&IR=T). Accessed 15 November, 2019.

Storr, W. (2018) *Selfie: How the West Became Self-obsessed*, London: Picador.

Storrie, C. (2006) *The Delirious Museum: A Journey from the Louvre to Las Vegas*, London: I.B. Tauris.

Subramanian, S. (2017) How to sell a city: the booming business of place branding, *The Guardian*, 7 November.

Sundbo, J. and Sørensen, F. (2013) Introduction to the experience economy, in J. Sundbo and F. Sørensen (eds) *Handbook on the Experience Economy*, Cheltenham: Edward Elgar Publishing.

Sweney, M. (2018) In with the old? While teenagers flee, over-55s flock to join Facebook, *The Guardian*, 12 February.

Swingewood, A. (1977) *The Myth of Mass Culture*, Basingstoke: Macmillan.

Sze Tsung Leong (2011) And then there was shopping, in *Harvard Design School Guide to Shopping: Project on the City 2*, directed by Rem Koolhaas, New York: Taschen.

Tapscott, D. and Williams, A. D. (2006) *Wikinomics: How Mass Collaboration Changes Everything*. New York: Portfolio.

Taylor, T. R. (2018) *Watch Me Play: Twitch and the Rise of Game Live Streaming*, Oxford: Princeton University Press.

Theodoridis, K., Miles, S. and Albertson, K. (2019) Negotiating reality through the presumption of the 'unreal' self: young people's identities in an age of economic precarity, in E. Colombo and P. Rebughini (eds) *Youth and the Politics of the Present: Coping with Complexity and Ambivalence*, London: Routledge.

Thomas, N. (2016) *The Return of Curiosity: What Museums are Good for in the 21st Century*, London: Reaktion Books.

Thompson, C. J. and Arsel, Z. (2004) The Starbucks brandscape and consumers' (anticorporate) experiences of glocalization, *Journal of Consumer Research*, 31(3), 631–42.

Thompson, J. (1990) *Ideology and Modern Culture*, Cambridge: Polity Press.

Thompson, N. (2016) *Culture as Weapon: The Art of Influence in Everyday Life*, London: Melville.

Thrift, N. (2006) Re-inventing invention: new tendencies in capitalist commodification, *Economy and Society*, 35(2), 279–306.

Tietze, S. and Musson, G. (2010) Identity, identity work and the experience of working from home, *Journal of Management Development*, 29(2), 148–56.

Toffler, A. (1981) *The Third Wave*, New York: Bantam Books.

Toffoletti, K. and Thorpe, H. (2017) The athletic labour of femininity: the branding and consumption of global celebrity sportswomen on Instagram, *Journal of Consumer Culture*, 18(2), 298–316.

Tolentino, J. (2019) *Trick Mirror: Reflection on Self-Delusion*, London: Fourth Estate.

Touraine, A. (1974) *The Post-Industrial Society*, London: Wildwood House.

Tuan, Y.-F. (1982) *Segmented Worlds and Self: Group Life and Individual Consciousness*, Minneapolis: University of Minnesota Press.

Tuan, Y.-F. (1998) *Escapism*, Baltimore: John Hopkins University Press.

Turkle, S. (2011) *Alone Technology: Why We Expect More from Technology and Less from Ourselves*, New York: Basic Books.

Tweedle, D. (2013) Making sense of insecurity: a defence of Richard Sennett's sociology of work, *Work, Employment and Society*, 27(1), 94–104.

Urry, J. (1990) *The Tourist Gaze: Leisure and Travel in Contemporary Society*, London: Sage.

Uusitalo, L. (1998) Consumption in postmodernity: social structuration and the construction of self, in M. Bianchi (ed.) *The Active Consumer: Novelty and Surprise in Consumer Choice*, London: Routledge.

Van Bowen, L. and Gilovich, T. (2003) To do or to have? That is the question, *Journal of Personality and Social Psychology*, 85, 1193–202.

Van Dijck, J., Poeel, T. and de Waal, M. (2018) *The Platform Society: Public Values in a Connective World*, Oxford: Oxford University Press.

Venkatraman, M. and Nelson, T. (2008) From servicescape to consumption-scape: a photo-elicitation study of Starbucks in the New China, *Journal of International Business Studies*, 39, 1010–26.

Von Hantelmann, D. (2014) *The Experiential Turn*, https://walkerart.org/collections/publications/performativity/experiential-turn/. Accessed 15 November 2019.

Wallman, J. (2013) *Stuffocation: Living More with Less*, London: Penguin Books.

Warde, A. (2005) Consumption and theories of practice, *Journal of Consumer Culture*, 5(2), 131–53.

Weber, M. (2002) *The Protestant Ethic and the Spirit of Capitalism*, London: Penguin.

Weeks, K. (2011) *The Problem of Work: Feminism, Marxism, Anti-work Politics and Post-work Imaginaries*, London: Duke University Press.

Westerbeek, H. and Smith, A. (2003) *Sport in the Global Market Place*, Basingstoke: Palgrave.

Whannel, G. (1992) *Fields in Vision: Television Sport and Cultural Transformation*, London: Routledge.

Williams, R. (1990) Base and Superstructure in Marxist Cultural Theory, in R. Williams, *Problems in Materialism and Culture*, London: Verso, 31–49.

Willis, P. (1978) *Learning to Labour: How Working Class Kids Get Working Class Jobs*, Aldershot: Ashgate.

Willis, S. (1991) *A Primer for Daily Life*, London: Routledge.

Wilson, R. (2007) *Theodor Adorno*, London: Routledge.

Wood, Z. (2017) Showbiz turns shopping into theatre of dreams, *The Guardian*, 28 October.

Yodanis, C. (2006) A place in town: doing class in a coffee shop, *Journal of Contemporary Ethnography*, 35(3), 341–66.

York, P. (2014) *Authenticity is a Con*, London: Biteback.

Zajc, M. (2015) Social media, presumption, and dispositives: new mechanisms of the construction of subjectivity, *Journal of Consumer Culture*, 15(1), 28–47.

Žižek, S. (2006) *How to Read Lacan*, New York: Newton.

Žižek, S. (2014) Slavloj Žižek on Coca-Cola, YouTube, 28 May, www.youtube.com/watch?v=zxraW7h4BJU. Accessed 15 November 2019.

Zuboff, S. (2019) *The Age of Surveillance Capitalism: The Fight for a Human Future at the New Frontier of Power*, New York: Public Affairs.

Zukin, S. (1991) *Landscapes of Power: From Detroit to Disney World*, London: University of California Press.

Index

Thanks to our Patreon Subscribers:

Abdul Alkalimat
Andrew Perry

Who have shown their generosity and comradeship in difficult times.

Check out the other perks you get by subscribing to our Patreon – visit patreon.com/plutopress.

Subscriptions start from £3 a month.

Printed and bound by CPI Group (UK) Ltd, Croydon, CR0 4YY

23/04/2025

14661020-0001